# Listen to This

**Developing an Ear for Expository**

**Marcia S. Freeman**

MAUPIN

HOUSE

Marcia S. Freeman is a writer and consultant specializing in the practical aspects of creating a classroom writing community. She is the author of *Building a Writing Community: A Practical Guide* (Maupin House 1995). Ms. Freeman appreciates comments and suggestions. Please write her care of the publisher.

Editor: *Candace Nelson*
Book and cover design: *Billie J. Hermansen*

Freeman, Marcia S. (Marcia Sheehan), 1937-
     Listen to this : developing an ear for expository / by Marcia S.
Freeman.
          p.     cm.
     Includes bibliographical references (p.  ).
     ISBN 0-929895-19-3
     1. English language—Composition and exercises—Study and teaching
(Elementary)     2. Exposition (Rhetoric)     I. Title.
LB1576.F729     1997
372.62'3'044—dc21                                                          97-4166
                                                                                 CIP

Maupin House Publishing, Inc.
P. O. Box 90148
Gainesville, FL  32607-0148
1-800-524-0634
jgraddy@maupinhouse.com

Maupin House publishes classroom-proven language arts resources for innovative teachers K-12. Call or write for a free catalogue.

10 9 8 7 6 5 4 3 2 1

# Listen to This: Developing an Ear for Expository

This resource for teachers and parents of developing writers, grades four through twelve, includes an expository writing primer, read-aloud samples with accompanying analysis notes, and a list of expository literature sources.

# Dedication

This book is dedicated to all the writers of graceful expository prose who granted me permission to reprint their work, and to my husband who was my principal editor.

# Preface

Almost everything almost everyone writes is exposition — communicating ideas and opinions, presenting and interpreting information, explaining, persuading, amusing. Done well, this writing is lively and exciting. Yet, teachers tell me their students prefer to write stories rather than expository pieces. When they ask me how they can encourage their students in expository writing, I tell them, "A good place to start is to **develop your students' ear for expository**." I wrote *Listen to This* to provide a source of information and materials teachers may use to accomplish this objective.

# Foreword

Writing education is receiving unprecedented emphasis in today's classrooms. Administrators and teachers are becoming increasingly aware that the art and science of writing is based on a body of knowledge that can be taught, to great effect. As a writing education consultant, I work with many of these administrators and teachers.

They commonly identify expository writing as a problem area. They tell me their students prefer to write stories rather than expository pieces. Fourth-grade teachers report that on state writing assessments their young writers do worse with expository prompts than narrative ones. During the course of addressing this problem with them, I conceived the thesis of this book, a thesis that has subsequently been validated in a large number of their classrooms.

If we read well-written expository pieces to our students regularly — asking them to listen for the specific expository characteristics and writing techniques that we have taught them — we can develop their ear for the genre and improve their expository writing skills dramatically. To this end, the book contains a broad variety of sample expository read-aloud pieces with accompanying notes that highlight the techniques each writer has used particularly well.

While the book's Expository Primer includes a good deal of concrete and practical information about the genre, I did not intend for it to be a complete and definitive work on expository writing. What I have included is enough to give teachers of developing writers a good initial source of expository writing target skills to teach in their classroom writing workshops. Ultimately, teachers will want to refer to the books listed in the bibliography in order to pick up additional techniques.

A word of caution. Reading and analyzing expository literature with your students, as an isolated practice, will not advance their writing skills. The exercise must be part of an ongoing classroom writing workshop. You need to teach the expository techniques your students will hear, in order for the reading and analysis to be effective. They will need to write many expository pieces, practicing the techniques illustrated and imitating the professionals.

Where I have recommended specific writing techniques, I have included explanations and examples. I find that many writing resource books instruct teachers to have their young writers use a particular technique and then omit explaining how to do it. "Always start your pieces with a *hook*, something to grab the readers attention," they advise, but nowhere do they reveal what a good hook might be. "Use *supporting details*," they counsel, but nowhere do they reveal what those supporting details are. I have tried to avoid that trap.

Marcia S. Freeman
April 1997

# Developing an Ear for Expository

You can help your students become better expository writers by regularly reading well-written, lively and amusing, people-centered expository literature to them. Children's listening vocabulary is larger than their reading vocabulary. They can understand material read to them that is well beyond their own reading ability. Take advantage of this.

As you read, call attention to the way the author handles the characteristics and techniques of expository writing. For example, point out an author's use of literary devices:

"Listen to this, kids. Comparisons all over the place. Here's one: *The pulp is as juicy as a mango's.* That's right, Mary Anne, it is a simile, and it sounds a lot like the one Mike used in his piece about mud and construction."

Point out the words an author uses to keep us moving forward or to let us know when the end is in sight:

"Listen to this, kids. The author keeps using the words *as well and in addition.* And at the end, he uses *remember* to remind us what he told us earlier about how to avoid the poison ivy."

Writing is a craft, and one of the best ways to learn a craft is to imitate the masters. If you visit the Metropolitan Museum of Art in New York, you will find students in front of their easels copying Van Dyck or Rubens, trying to create the effect of lace with oil paints, as those masters did. Budding artists, musicians, dancers, and athletes the world over imitate the pros and draw inspiration from them. Writers can do the same. We can copy the techniques of master writers.

The students in a second-grade class I visit regularly learned how the authors in Ranger Rick magazine love to start their articles with a question. What's the matter — don't you like *crunchy caterpillars on your pizza?* began a writer of a piece about edible bugs and their high protein content. *Can you imagine these smells? A pine forest after a rain. Cinnamon rolls in the oven. Your favorite shampoo. A rose bush in bloom.* began another writer in an article about how animals can smell chemical messages. (Fancy that, incomplete sentences!)

Now these second-graders love to start their expository pieces with, *Have you ever seen a manatee up close?* or *How big do you think a manatee is?* instead of *I am going to tell you three things about manatees,* or *Manatees are big.* By copying the pros, they added one more technique to their growing bank of writing skills, and their writing has become more graceful as a result.

## Reading Aloud

When we read to children, nine times out of ten we read fiction. While this helps them develop an ear for story, it inadvertently implies that expository writing is less interesting, less exciting, and less important than fiction. By neglecting to read expository literature, we miss the opportunity to help our students get a feeling and appreciation for the genre.

Just as students develop an ear and a preference for different styles of music, so can they develop an ear and preference for different genres of writing. You can help your students become better expository writers by reading well-written expository samples to them. Here are some guidelines:

- Initially, read **informational pieces** that deal with facts and concrete material. These are easier for children to analyze than essays, which deal with abstract concepts and opinions. Informational pieces provide good examples of organizational schemes and interesting beginnings and endings. When you read an informational expository sample to your students, have them identify where the writer starts each new clump of information.

  I love nature and science, so when I read to young writers, I often read from *Ranger Rick* magazine. Students not only hear how well-written science articles are constructed, but they pick up science information as well.

- Read **newspaper articles** that will have appeal to students. Your young writers will hear how journalists address who, what, where, and when, as quickly as possible.

- Read **humorists' columns**. Point out how these writers love to use hyperbole and non sequiturs. I particularly enjoy the way humor columnist David Grimes does it: *The first thing you need to know is that columnists are people, just like you, except that we're much smarter and <u>better looking</u>. So you should never be afraid to approach a columnist, <u>assuming you've had all your shots</u>.*

- Read **editorials and letters-to-the-editor**. These are usually **persuasive** in nature, the writer trying to convince the reader to adopt his point of view. They will contain examples of the types of arguments writers use in persuasive writing. In addition, they will demonstrate how writers back up their arguments with supporting details such as narrative vignettes, statistics, scientific facts, and authoritative quotes.

- Read from toy packages, snack food and clothing ads, travel brochures. All these try to **persuade** us to spend money. They use arguments that appeal to our vanity or emotions, and convince us of their products' benefits to our health, wealth, and social standing. *If you buy these shoes, you will jump like Michael Jordan.*

- Read game rules and directions for making or assembling things from recipe or craft books. These contain excellent **process descriptions** and the associated transition words. They demonstrate the imperative sentence construction peculiar to the genre: *First, fasten the T-shaped bar to Pipe A with one of the screws provided. Do not tighten it fully. Next, clip the bar to pipe B...*

- Most important, read expository pieces your students or other students have written.

## Student Samples Provide Powerful Models

When you use students' writing as models, you demonstrate that you value what they have to say and that professional writing is not the only source of good expository writing. You will find many examples of skillful expository writing in your own classroom. The precise use of just one characteristic or technique makes a student's piece a powerful sample.

I regularly carry children's writing with me as I travel from school to school. Recently, in a class of fourth-graders working on expository writing, I read one of my jewels, an informational piece in which the fourth-grade author described the ocean floor. He organized it by using natural divisions — the layers of the ocean floor. He used the transitional device of a descending diver to take the reader from paragraph to paragraph, from one ocean floor layer to another — *If you dive another 100 feet, you will come to the continental slope.*

When I finished reading the piece, a girl raised her hand and said, "That sounds like a *Magic School Bus* book!" She was right. He had imitated a pro, author Joanna Cole.

The teacher of this same class reported recently that the latest transitional device making its way through their active writing community is a tour guide approach to informational writing, as in: *Next, you can see... As you learn more about this, you will notice...* The students in this class have fun with their writing.

## Use Good Examples Over and Over

Whenever you find a good expository sample, reread it to your children during the year. Most professional samples exhibit many genre characteristics and techniques. They can do multiple duty. As students become familiar with the content, they can concentrate more easily on the author's techniques.

Team up with colleagues and develop a common file of samples to support the expository writing characteristics, components, and techniques that you all teach. Check children's magazines first. They contain a large variety of styles: book reviews, news, profiles of achievers, essays, articles, interviews, kids writing to kids, how-to articles, kids' opinions, etc. These pieces are usually short. Help each other analyze the samples and identify the characteristics and techniques each article demonstrates.

Look for pieces in which a strong focus is maintained; in which the author uses literary devices such as alliteration, simile, metaphor, hyperbole, onomatopoeia, and personification;

in which the author stresses the new, the up-to-date; in which the writing is people-centered; in which the author supports an argument with quotations — in short, pieces in which writers display the many wonderful and useful tools and techniques of the writing craft.

I guarantee a bonus: in the process *you* will learn a lot about expository writing.

## The Samples

The "Read-Aloud Samples" in this book are an array of expository pieces written by students, professional writers, and amateurs. The collection includes a wide range of expository literature: humorous essays, process descriptions, informational articles, opinion papers, persuasive essays, restaurant reviews, advertisements, letters-to-the-editor, and poetry.

The collection includes samples appropriate for different grades and writing skill levels. They are numbered and presented in order of increasing grade and level. The analysis notes accompanying each sample identify and describe the specific characteristics of good expository writing that the sample contains.

From this collection, select the pieces that best illustrate the expository writing skill(s) your students are currently studying and need to hear used. One highlighted skill is enough for the youngest students, but older children, with practice, can listen for one or two related skills. Use the accompanying analysis notes to help you choose relevant samples.

These samples will provide you with a good starting base for your read-aloud program. Ultimately, you will want to add to the collection. Following the samples section, you will find a bibliography of additional sources of read-aloud expository literature for elementary and middle/high school students.

Magazines are a good source of expository writing, and the pieces are generally short. Informational expository writing predominates. But you also will find opinions, book and movie reviews, letters-to-the-editor, interviews, how-to articles, and

occasionally, an essay. (Essays written specifically for elementary and middle school students are rare and hard to find.)

## Teaching Expository Techniques in Writing Workshop

Before you begin using the Read-Aloud Samples, you will want to review the next chapter, a primer describing the characteristics and techniques of expository writing. These include function, form, organization, transitions, supporting details, elaboration techniques, literary style, word usage, beginnings, and endings. Use this information to plan your writing workshop lessons and to help you select samples to read to your students.

The expository writing techniques I present in this primer can be used as target skills. That is, they will be the subject of your mini-lessons, the skills your students learn to apply in their practice pieces and their ongoing, independent writing. Later, you will have your students apply these target skills in an assessed piece.

Help your students become educated listeners. Combine reading aloud expository literature with teaching specific techniques and application practice. Your students will come to understand and appreciate the genre, and begin to master it.

In a school where I coach teachers in writing education, a class of fourth-graders was getting ready to write about rain forests, a theme in which they had been immersed for two weeks. As all writers do when faced with a writing assignment, they were wrestling with the problem of organization and presentation.

Most of the writers planned to present their ideas by clumping their information into the natural division of the rain forest — forest floor, understory, canopy, etc. But one student raised his hand and asked, "Remember, you read us an article called the ABCs of Computers? Can I present all the stuff I have in an ABCs of Rain Forests? I could go, A is for anteater and tell all about them, then B is for birds, C is for canopy, like that." A

classmate interrupted and said, "X will be hard to do."
Undaunted, the young writer answered, "I'll skip some letters,
or... I know, I'll just do the letters R, A, I, N, F, O, R, E, S, T, S."

Why not?

# An Expository Writing Primer

Expository writing should never be dull and uninteresting or so convoluted as to be beyond understanding. There is no reason for its authors to resort to jargon, to use long words when a short one will do, to avoid the use of the words *I* or *you*, to start every paragraph with a topic sentence, or to make each paragraph four to six sentences long (which so many school children tell me is the correct length).

Expository writing can, and should, be written in lively, clear, and interesting prose that engages the reader.

How do we help our students achieve this? By teaching them the characteristics and techniques that are peculiar to the genre; by reading well-written expository literature to them and pointing out how the authors use these characteristics and techniques; and by demonstrating how to use them in their own writing.

Let us consider some of the major characteristics and useful techniques of expository writing appropriate for young developing writers.

## General Characteristics and Techniques of Expository Writing

### Function

Expository writing seeks to inform, explain, teach, persuade, or amuse.

## Forms

Expository writing goes by many informal names, such as essay, report, theme, review, and opinion paper. Some people inappropriately call it *non-fiction.* We must be careful not to use *non-fiction* as a synonym for expository writing. Narrative writing can also be non-fictional — for example, a story about your family's outing. The best way to avoid confusing young writers is to refer to each kind of expository writing by its specific name: literature response, book review, opinion paper, business letter, persuasive essay, invitation, etc.

The expository genre includes two basic forms. One is informational writing, which often includes explanation. It deals with concrete facts. Examples may include process description, informative articles, directions, advertisements, news reports, and business letters.

The other form, essay (also known as exposition), deals with abstract concepts or ideas, and opinions. Examples may include business letters, letters-to-the-editor, editorials, speeches, persuasive essays, and restaurant, book, drama, dance, and art reviews. With the essay, we present and develop ideas. As we write, we find out what we know and what we want to say. Writing, thinking, and learning become one.

Some forms of expository writing exhibit characteristics and techniques unique to that form. For example, a business letter requires a special format and a humorous essay relies on special word usage. Most of the characteristics and techniques of expository writing, however, apply to all or most of the forms.

## Organization

Exposition is organized in clumps of related information or ideas. Narration, in contrast, is organized chronologically to show the passage of time.

## Focus

Good expository writing is focused and unified, which means it is all about one subject. The reader must be able to find the main idea of the piece and follow its development. The main idea must be supported by examples and details that lie within the reader's experience.

Writers build cohesion or unity within a piece by using techniques such as maintaining a consistent point of view, adhering to parallel construction, using effective transitions, and repeating key words and phrases.

## Clarity

I heard some excellent writing advice from prolific free-lance writer, lecturer, and college professor, Dr. Dennis Hensley. He pointed out that the expository author must write not only to be understood, but so that there is no chance he will be misunderstood.

If a reader cannot understand what is written, it is almost always the writer's fault. Consider this interesting tidbit from newspaper article: *"Few details emerged Wednesday about the crash, which authorities said involved an experienced driver and one of Florida's largest."* Did the writer mean to comment on the size of the driver? We usually know what we want to say; we have to make sure we say it clearly.

## Lively and People Oriented

Expository writing should be lively. Narrative passages — little stories or anecdotes about people and events — bring life to a piece, illustrating ideas and helping the reader understand the thesis. People want to read about people, not things. Including people in a piece engages the reader. An effective expository writer names people, describes them, quotes them: *When I was a kid, my mother was forever yelling at me, "Don't run with those scissors,"* instead of, *It is dangerous to run with scissors.*

Writers engage their readers by talking directly to them; *You will succeed*, instead of, *One will succeed.* Good writers say what they think, using the word 'I': *Correct me if I am wrong...*

Expository writers should make use of all the effective literary devices and descriptive techniques found in the narrative genre.

# Target Skills

The expository writing techniques that your young, developing writers need should be the target skills you teach in your classroom writing workshop. A target skill is the subject of a mini-lesson. Students practice using the target skill during the lesson and they revisit the concept in group lessons with you. They listen for the target skill in the read-aloud samples and hear how writers apply it. They practice using the target skill in their independent writing such as journals or ongoing pieces headed for publication or their portfolios. Finally, they show off their use of the target skill in a prompted or assigned expository piece that you will assess.[1]

## Organizational Schemes

A narrative is relatively easy to follow. It's a bit like learning the words to a song. In a song, the melody helps us remember the words. In a narrative, the passage of time or plot line helps us follow the action.

Expository writing can be more difficult for a reader to follow. It deals with ideas and information that are not linked by time. Its writers must impose order — devise a plan — to help their readers deal with the information and follow their ideas. Fortunately, there are a number of established ways to do that. All utilize some form of clumping related information and ideas.

Here are some useful schemes that developing writers can understand and apply.

- Logical order based on natural divisions within the topic.
    A report or informational article. Examples — Baseball
    Elements: rules, players, equipment, field; Rain
    Forest Layers: canopy, understory, forest floor, etc.
- Sequential order presenting step-by-step information and description.
    Process description: how to make or do something.
    Giving directions: how to get somewhere.

---

[1] Marcia S. Freeman, Building a Writing Community: A Practical Guide (Florida, Maupin House Publishing, 1995), 96

- Hierarchy of ideas based on importance or logic.

  Explanation: building a general concept through presentation of the components, the specifics.

  Persuasive essay: arguments building up to the clincher.

- Alphabetical order.

  Informational writing: the ABCs of a topic to give readers an overview.

- Comparison, using differences and similarities to advance a thesis or to explain.

  Literature analysis by comparison: characters in a book.

Choosing an organizational scheme for a piece requires identifying the potential or intended audience. Writers need to consider their readers' background knowledge. Knowing that will help them determine which scheme to use. For instance, "The ABCs of the Rain Forest" might be great for fourth-grade readers who are studying the topic for the first time, while a comparison between the rain forests of Costa Rica and Northern California might be more appropriate for environmental science students.

In writing workshop, show your students how to organize their writing in the variety of ways appropriate to their age and experience. Most developing writers, of any age, do best trying out concrete means of organization first — such as clumping related information into natural divisions — before trying to organize by a hierarchy based on logic or importance, or by comparison. ( See Appendix II, "Lesson: Organizing an informational piece by physically clumping related information.")

Read expository samples to your students that illustrate a variety of organizational schemes. Help your students recognize and categorize them. (See Samples # 1, 5, 7, 9, 15, 17.)

## Supporting Details

Recently, I tutored a junior from a gifted-and-talented high school program. She was having difficulty with expository writing. All the papers she brought with her were marked in red, "Needs more supporting details."

When I was a student writer, my papers consistently came back marked exactly the same way. At that time, I thought writing was some magical skill that only a few gifted persons and the English teacher could lay claim to. So I never ventured to ask about supporting details. But this frustrated high school junior did, asking me, almost in tears, **"WHAT ARE THEY!"**

Here are some, with student-written examples of their use.

- Real life examples

    *Aunts are not always as old as your parents. My Aunt Katrina is two years younger than I am! My mother was 24 and had two kids (including me) when her mother, my grandmother, had Katrina.*

- Descriptive details

    *You can tell the difference between the United States' coins by feel. The fifty-cent piece, the quarter, and the dime all have grooved edges, and the nickel and penny have smooth edges. The coins are each a different size and thickness.*

- Authoritative quotes and citations (For young writers, the authority can be a parent, teacher, friend, coach, relative, neighbor.)

    *I would like to have a pet. My grandmother always says, "Taking care of a pet makes you responsible."*

- Numbers or statistics

    *We should have a traffic light by the library. When we try to cross from school it is dangerous. Last year we saw three accidents at that corner, and one kid was hit on his bike.*

- Proofs

    *I am good at swimming. Last year, in the first swim meet I ever entered, I won a first-place trophy.*

- Specific examples

    *Friends are loyal, and you can trust them. If you tell your friend a secret, she will not tell anyone else.*

- Definitions

    *I am good at karate. It is a Japanese martial art.*

*An Expository Writing Primer*

- Anecdotes

    *Winds can do a lot of damage. My friend Joshua lived in Homestead, and when the hurricane hit, all the houses on his block lost their roofs.*

- Allusions

    *It reminds me of the feeling you get just before a storm. Everything is kind of still, like we're all waiting for something to happen. It's a funny feeling.*

- Comparisons and analogies

    *Kids go to school like grownups go to work. They both have jobs. Kids have to learn things, and grownups have to do things or make things.*

- Self-evident truths

    *I hate girls. Our teacher makes us pick girls for computer partners. <u>They are not like boy partners</u>. They giggle too much.*

## Focus

Focus means that a piece is all about one subject, that the subordinate parts are related, and that the writer does not wander off the topic. It means the piece contains no extraneous material; no *left-field sentences*, no extra ideas.

By left-field sentence, I mean a sentence that does not belong, a non sequitur. For example:

> *Parrots are found in Central and South America. Rain forests are their natural habitat. Their diet consists chiefly of fruit and seeds. **My Aunt Polly has a parrot.** Parrots are noted for their colorful feathers.*

Extra ideas are an extension of left-field sentences and represent a loss of focus. Young writers may start to tell their readers about one thing, then wander off to another idea. These wanderings commonly are spotted when young writers read their pieces aloud in peer conferences.

Encourage your young writers to write the name of the topic at the top of each rough-draft page — *This is about whales and what they eat. This is about my gymnastics class. This is about honor and loyalty.*

They can do the same for each paragraph: *This paragraph is about what whales eat. This paragraph is about where whales are found.* This technique will help them stay focused.

After you read the first paragraph of an expository sample, have your students identify what the piece is about. Then, have them listen to how the author stays **focused** on that topic. Ask them several times during the reading, "Is the writer still on the topic? How does this section relate to the topic?" (See Samples # 1, 2, 4, 7, 13, 15.)

## Lively Writing

If we want readers to enjoy our writing and recommend it to others, it has to be lively. By lively writing, I do not mean overly informal writing with a casual tone. When we tell young writers, "Write the way you talk," we do not mean for them to use jargon or street slang such as *go* for *says,* or *Me and Jason* for *Jason and I.* We mean for them to write in the active voice, tell stories to make a point, use creative phrases, and refer to specific people, just as they do in speaking. What we are after is precise writing that is colorful and informative.

Following are some techniques that will help your students achieve lively writing. Young writers can understand and apply these techniques. They may not, particularly at first, put them all together in one piece, but they will start to use many of them after they learn about them. Teach these techniques as target skills in writing workshop, and follow up by reading expository literature that demonstrates their use.

1. Talk to the reader.

Teachers often tell me that when they wrote expository pieces in elementary and high school they were told to avoid the word *I*. Modern writing experts unanimously agree that this is poor advice. (Who knows where these rules came from?)

William Zinsser[2], in *Writing to Learn* tells about John Rodgers, a distinguished professor of geology at Yale, who became so maddened by a fuzzy student dissertation that he wrote

---

[2] William Zinsser, *Writing to Learn,* (New York: Harper & Row, Publishers, 1988). 80.

and distributed to his class a tongue-in-cheek manifesto called "Rules of Bad Writing." Among these rules was: *Never use the first person, (I), where you can use ambiguous phrases like "the writer" or, "it is thought" or, better still, "it is considered by some," so the reader can't be exactly sure who thinks what, or what — if anything — **you** think.*

Writers should not hesitate to use the word *you*, even in a serious academic piece. In "The Geological History of Connecticut," a piece about radiometric dating of meteorites, Professor Rodgers writes: *If you think the earth and the moon formed at the same time, you would conclude that the earth is 4.6 billion years old.*[3] Readers enjoy it when the author talks directly to them — they are engaged.

2. <u>Use the active voice.</u>

Nothing kills the liveliness of an expository piece as quickly as the use of the passive voice. If your reader has to ask, "Who is doing what to whom?" you are in the passive voice — and you are in trouble. And yet, as soon as we think we need to sound official, most of us resort to a stilted, passive-voice syntax. We write, *It has been decided that bicycles must be parked in the bike corral,* instead of *The principal and faculty ask that students park their bicycles only in the bike corral.*

Consider which of the following accounts of a game that sports fans would prefer to read in their newspaper. *The winning team was determined in the ninth inning when the pitch was made and it was hit for a home run.* Or, *Jason Peters won the game for the Cougars when he hit Ron Bower's ninth-inning pitch into the stands.*

Teach your young writers to make a person, a doer, the subject of their sentences. Remember, people want to read about people, not things.

Examples: Passive: *Report cards will be distributed.* Active: *Your teacher will hand out report cards.* Passive: *The cans of food are collected on Mondays.* Active: *School children collect canned food on Mondays.*

---

[3] op. cit. 87.

One dead giveaway of the passive voice are verbs with help-ers. *Report cards will be distributed. Bicycles must be parked.* Another giveaway is the word *by.* Say bye, bye to all those *bys.* Richard Lanham,[4] in *Revising Business Prose,* says the acid test is the question, "Who's kicking who?" If a sentence doesn't answer that question explicitly, it's written in the passive voice.

Young developing writers write naturally in the active voice. Around high school, however, students start to use the passive voice. This may be in response to archaic rules of writing they have heard through the years such as, "Don't use *I* or *you* in expository writing," or, the many unfortunate examples of *officialese* they have come across in bulletins, newsletters, and such. When students think that their writing has to sound academic, formal, and authoritative, they lose their natural voice and produce the stilted and fuzzy expository writing Professor Rodgers so abhors.

Zinsser[5] points out, "It's a fact of the publishing industry that at least 90% of the manuscripts that academics submit for general publication are too poorly written to be considered. Their language is a language squeezed dry of human juice — a Sargasso Sea of passive verbs, long and generalized nouns, pompous locution, and unnecessary jargon."

3. Use narrative vignettes.

Narrative vignettes or anecdotes are effective in expository writing. These "little stories" can provide strong support for ideas. They make the writing come alive, they make it people centered, they engage the reader. You are likely to find narrative bits in most well-written expository pieces other than business letters, directions, and (most) advertisements.

A fourth-grader's response to an expository prompt about the impact of weather provides a good example. *Weather affects us all. The effects can be good or bad. One thing bad is a big wind, like in a blizzard. When I lived in Maine, we had a blizzard one winter. The wind was so bad it blew the sheet metal roof off our barn. My dad had to put tarps over the holes until spring.*

---

[4] Richard Lanham, *Revising Business Prose,* (Charles Scribner's Sons: New York, 1981) 1.

[5] Zinsser, 183.

Students need to recognize the difference between a willy-nilly mixing of expository and narrative styles and the deliberate use of a bit of narrative to support and enliven exposition. Wandering aimlessly between narrative and expository style is sloppy writing.

4. Be specific.

One of the joys of reading is recognizing the familiar — "I feel that way too! I've noticed that very same thing." Specificity is the tool good writers use to bring that joy to readers. They always favor the specific over the general. Not: *I went to the store,* but: *I went to K-Mart.* Not: *I admire my teacher because she is nice,* but, the specific: *I admire my teacher because she treats all the kids fairly.* Make specificity a target skill.

(The vocabulary of writing workshop can pop up in the strangest places. In a second-grade class I visited, the children had been working hard on specificity. A child wrote in her whale report: *Whales live in the Spacific Ocean.*)

5. Choose words carefully.

The short, simple, and familiar:

Virtually all experts agree: good writers choose the simplest and shortest word that suits their purpose; good writers use long, exotic, or obscure words only when those words are required to clearly express their meaning — and good writers make certain they use exotic words correctly.

> *Note: This principle, preferring the short or common word to the long or obscure word, is included for you as a writer and for advanced writing students. Young developing writers need to be encouraged to develop their vocabulary. Many children love big words, and if we discourage them, they might feel inhibited about trying to use them.

Joseph A. Ecclesine[6] had fun demonstrating the principle of short words in his essay, "Big Words Are For The Birds." He writes:

*"When you come right down to it, there is no law that says you <u>have</u> to use big words when you write or talk.*

*There are lots of small words, and good ones, that can be made to say all the things you want to say, quite as well as the big ones. It may take a bit more time to find them at first, but it can be well worth it (since we all know what they mean).*

*Small words can be crisp, brief, terse — they go right to the point, like a knife. They have a charm all their own. They dance, twist, turn, and sing. Like sparks in the night they light the way for the eyes of those who read. They are the grace notes of prose..."*

To prove his point, he wrote the entire essay using words of one syllable.

Appropriate words:

Thoughtful writers choose words that are appropriate for their audience. They select words that create the desired tone of their piece. If students write a persuasive essay to the school board or to their principal to advocate changing a school policy, they would not use the vocabulary they use when they talk with their friends. An informative and enlightening exercise for older students is to write the same persuasive essay to two vastly different audiences. For example, they might write to convince the school board that school uniforms would be a good idea. Then, write to convince their classmates.

Word values and impact:

Smart writers select words for their value and impact as well as their meaning. They are careful that the words they choose do not offend or antagonize their audience. Aside from their dictionary meaning (denotative), words have connotative values, both negative and positive. For example, *computer geek* and *old*

---

[6] Joseph A. Ecclesine, "Big Words Are For The Birds," *Printer's Ink*, February 17, (1961).

*geezer* have negative connotations while *computer ace* and *senior citizen* have positive connotations.

Words have emotive values too. If we want to stir people's emotions, we cannot use bland language. To convince the county transportation department that we need a new traffic light on a corner, we do not say, "Kids are *getting hurt* there," we say, "There's *carnage* at that corner."

6.   Use a variety of sentence construction and length.

Gary Provost[7], in his classic writer's guide, *100 Ways To Improve Your Writing,* shows us why we need to vary our sentence length. *This sentence has five words. Here are five more words. Five-word sentences are fine. But several together become monotonous. Listen to what is happening. The writing is getting boring. The sound of it drones. It's like a stuck record.*

Developing writers can check their writing for sentence length variety by counting the number of words in each sentence of their draft. If a pattern, such as 7, 6, 8, 6, 7, 7, 6, 6, 7 emerges, they should look for a way to remedy it.

One remedy is to expand some sentences by adding details that answer one of the following questions: where, why, how, when, which one. For example, from Sample #18, "Big Words Are For The Birds": *There are lots of small words that can be made to say all the things you want to say, quite as well as the big ones.* The addition, *quite as well as the big ones,* answers the question, *how.*

These additions are not always tacked on the end of the sentence. Here is an example from Sample #5, "Another Rabbit." *I'm sure by the end of my letter I will have convinced you.* The student writer added a few words in the middle of a sentence to tell the reader *when.* Listen to how many of these expanded sentences are demonstrated in Sample #11, "Soaring With Books."

---

[7] Gary Provost, *100 Ways to Improve Your Writing,* (New American Library: New York, 1985), 61

Combining two sentences is another way to create longer sentences. The writers must be careful that the two sentences are closely related. For instance, these two sentences from Gary Provost's example cannot be combined gracefully: *Listen to what is happening. The writing is getting boring.* These two, on the other hand, can: *The sound of it drones. It's like a stuck record.* Try it.

> Note: Combining sentences is no remedy for very young writers. They already tend to connect so many ideas with "and" that we spend a great deal of time training them to break up the long strands into separate sentences.

## Beginnings

Ask any writer. The all-important first sentence of a piece of writing is often the hardest to compose. Many of us get around this problem by writing the body of the piece first, then going back to write the first sentence and the first paragraph. At that point, we know what our piece is about and where we want to lead our readers.

Once we know what it's about and how it's organized, we can compose an appropriate beginning. And after that, we can write a wonderful hook. In essence we're going backwards: First the body of the piece, then the introduction, then the first words.

Beginnings can be one line, one paragraph, or several paragraphs. The content often determines which kind of a beginning fits. Here are some of the kinds of beginnings young writers find useful:

- giving topic background information
- telling how they became interested in the topic
- telling how they feel about the subject
- telling why the topic is important to the reader
- revealing their plan of presentation
- enumerating the main points of the topic.

If you write about a personal hobby, you might choose to tell how you got interested in it or how you feel about it. If you write a letter-to-the-editor about the traffic in your neighborhood, you might choose to give background information about the problem. If you write about the dangers of catching the flu, you might choose to tell your readers how important this topic is to them. After you have written the body of your piece, you usually will know which one to choose.

Once you decide on the introductory paragraph scheme, you can address the all important first sentence(s). You need for it to be a *hook* that quickly gets your reader's attention, using words that will entice him to read on. To that end, the hook should be easy to read. It can take many forms. Sometimes it is the title, sometimes it is the first few words or sentences. There are no rules.

Here are some hooks professionals use that young writers can try out.

| Hook | Example |
|------|---------|
| Question | What? You don't like crunchy caterpillars on your pizza? |
| Idiom (figure of speech) | Now you're in a pickle. No food, no water, no shelter. What do you do? |
| Anecdote (narrative vignette) | I was living in Arkansas the first time I met prejudice face to face. |
| Definition | Hyperbole means extreme exaggeration. I found out it was easier to say than use. |
| Exaggeration (hyperbole) | A billion bikers can't be wrong. |
| Setting | In a small school, tucked up in a hollow in Kentucky, students are discovering the power of excellence. |
| Quotation | "Give me liberty or give me death." |
| Pun: a play on words. | Now, spider-silk crosshairs are spinning out of existence. |
| A riddle | What do you call an eight-legged weaver? |

| Hook | Example |
|---|---|
| Alliterative phrase | Stepping and stomping. Whirling and swirling. To the Native American Dance Troop these moves are the key to their art. |
| Words in capitals, bold or italics | STOP! LOOK! LISTEN! The safety patrol wants you. |
| Exclamation | Whew! And you thought the desert was hot! |
| Noises (onomatopoeia) | Slurp, slurp. Glug, glug. On a hot day the best thing to quench your thirst is a tasty fruit drink from Holler Hollow Snack Bar. |
| Sentence fragments | A rose in full-bloom. Your favorite perfume. A steak cooking over charcoal. Our sense of smell tells us plenty. |
| General to specific statement | When we talk of honor, we need to start with honesty. |
| Name of famous person or place | Judy Bloom will never know what she started. |
| Quaint, archaic, foreign or obscure term | "It's déja vu, all over again." Yogi Berra is a wordsmith extraordinaire. |
| Reference to money | All it takes is pennies a day and you can become a millionaire in a year. |

In writing workshop, invite your students to copy the pros when they start their expository pieces. How about a question? Or a noise? Read expository literature to them that illustrates the many and varied beginnings that professional writers use.

Have students collect first lines of expository writing from magazines, newspapers, and advertisements. They should sort them into categories, such as the ones I have listed, and put them in their writer's notebook to use as models in their own writing.

## Endings

Simply put, the function of an effective ending is to wrap it up. Endings that hark back to the same style as the beginning are very effective. One way to do this is to begin the final paragraph in the same fashion as the beginning, using a variation of the hook.

Here is an example. A sixth-grader began her piece with *Reading takes you places you'd never go,* and then commenced to write about her love affair with books. She ended with *Reading brings you friends you'd never know,* her final reason why she is hooked on books and a rhyming echo of her hook.

Concrete models of ending paragraphs are helpful to developing writers. The following endings work for most intermediate, middle school, and high school students.

- Remind the reader of the main idea.
- Reiterate, or restate, how you feel about the subject.
- Draw a conclusion from the list of ideas, examples, or arguments.
- Raise a further question about the subject.
- Invite the reader to learn more: provide a reference as to where.
- Present the clincher, the strongest argument in a persuasive piece.
- Reiterate, or restate, the main points. Be careful not to hit your readers over the head. The reiteration or restatement must be subtle, not: *I have told you the three reasons I love books.*

Remember that writing a summary is difficult for young developing writers. The classic speechmaker's strategy — "Tell them what you are going to say, say it, then tell them what you said" — is not such a good idea for them. Young writers, who take things literally, interpret this advice to mean that they should write the same thing three times. Older students who use the advice end up hitting their readers over the head. Readers do not need to be told what they just read.

Here are some professional examples of opening sentences to an ending paragraph. Students can use these as models.

- Reminder statement

    *Be sure to look for the tell-tale rings on the tree . . .*
    *Remember that not all snakes are . . .*

- Finality or Eventuality

    *The last thing you need to know is where to find . . .*
    *The last thing to do is deliver it to . . .*

- Quotation concerning topic

    *"Let us all join in preserving the . . ."*
    *"I owe my success to . . ."*
    *"I hope you will be inspired by this to . . ."*

- Author's feelings

    *The thing I liked best about Girl Scout camp . . .*
    *I knew then I would always be happy in . . .*
    *This valuable information helped me realize my goal . . .*

- Predictions

    *The next time you go diving, you will know how to . . .*
    *In no time at all, you will be able to reach . . .*

- Summary Statement

    *To survive, they must . . . , . . . , and . . .*
    *No matter how you look at it, the last thing you want . . .*

- An invitation to the reader

    *Next time you are surrounded by darkness . . . look up and imagine . . .*
    *So, if you find yourself in an argument about policy, try . . .*

- Reference to more on the topic

    *For more details. . . .*
    *Send a self-addressed postcard to . . .*

## Transitions

The transitions that writers use depend on the organizational scheme of their piece. In narrative writing, time and place orienters help readers find their way. In expository writing, words that tie ideas together or that signal a new step in a process lead readers through the information and ideas. Transitions can be used within a sentence, within a paragraph, or **between paragraphs**.

Writing transitions **between paragraphs** is one of the most difficult skills for novice and experienced writers. Very often, instead of using a transition word, writers choose a different way to relate one paragraph to another. They take a word or phrase that ended one paragraph and begin the next paragraph with that same word or phrase. I just did that. I repeated the phrase, *"between paragraphs,"* from the prior paragraph, in the first sentence of this paragraph.

Transitions often are not needed between paragraphs. The organization of a piece may lead a reader from point to point without requiring a transition to start a paragraph. (See Sample #15, "How The Stock Market Works.") Or, the organization might be in the form of a list which does not require transitions. (See Sample #17, "Don't Run With Those Scissors.")

The best approach to teaching expository transitions is to teach young writers how to use them within paragraphs first, as illustrated in some of the following examples, then move on to between-paragraph transitions.

Elementary school writers have little trouble replacing their *and thens* in narrative with time-orienters, once they know some of them and hear how often professional writers use them in fiction. These transitions very often signal the start of a new paragraph. Students can find lots of them easily in the fiction they read by checking the first word or two at each paragraph indentation.

Similarly, in expository writing, young writers find the easiest transitions to use are the sequential ones associated with process description: *first, next, after you . . . , the last step,* etc. They also can handle transitions of incidence: *sometimes, always, never.* More difficult for them are the transitions of addition. Show your intermediate students how to use additive transitions in persuasive pieces in which they add argument after argument.

Continue to point out transitions to your student when you read sample pieces aloud. Teach specific transition types or specific transition words within their associated form. At the appropriate age or writing skill-level of your students, make transitions a target skill. It is a critical skill that gives a written piece cohesion.

- Additions: and, also, or, along with, again, similarly, for instance, for example, for one thing, for another thing, especially, altogether, besides, in addition, . . .

*Sports do not all require the same skills.* **For instance**, *running a marathon doesn't require the coordination that basketball does.* **And**, *playing ping pong doesn't require the muscle strength of wrestling.*

- Alternatives: on the other hand, or, whereas, but, while, . . .

    *Choosing a pet is difficult.  There are so many animals that make good pets. Dogs make good pets.  They're loyal, they almost can talk to you.  They can do things for you such as pulling you in a sled, carrying things, and warning you of danger.*

    **On the other hand**, *cats are easier to care for.  You don't have to walk or wash them.  You can leave them for several days because they don't eat all their food at once.*

- Cause and effect: as a result, because, which caused, that resulted in, what happened was, which produced, naturally, therefore, . . .

    *Voter turnout is an important part of the equation. A low turnout can result in a bias toward one party.* **As a result**, *something as unrelated to politics as the weather can affect the composition of Congress.*

- Comparisons (similarities and differences): like, similarly, in a similar fashion, as with, just as, both, unlike, whereas, however, on the other hand, in which case, or, whereas, but, . . .

    *Zebras are a lot like horses.  They* **both** *have hooves and have* **similar** *teeth,* **the same** *shaped body and head. The zebra,* **however**, *does not have a mane.*

    **Like** *horses, zebras lives in herds, grazing for grass on the plains.*

- Emphasis:  again, to repeat, for this reason, to emphasize, truly, in fact, as I said, to reiterate, . . .

    *I do not think we should have recess at the same time as the kindergartners. We are bigger and we get in trouble if we knock them over or don't give them the swings. We could share the playground with the fifth graders.*

    **In fact**, *none of the big kids should be on the play-ground with the kindergartners. Big kids should be with big kids.*

- Incidence: always, usually, frequently, occasionally, sometimes, never, . . .

    *You will love this school. We are always going on field trips. **Usually** they are educational. Last year we went to the ballet and the opera.*

    ***Sometimes** we go on field trips that are just for fun, like the zoo. We even went to a real circus, under a tent.*

- Progression: first, second, third, last, now, then, until, finally, later, afterward, when, until, not until, eventually, meanwhile, immediately, soon, at last, the last thing, . . .

    *If you want to make a great sandwich, try this. **First**, heat up a pita bread. **Then**, slice a tomato very thin. Cut the pita bread open along one side. **Next**, put lettuce, tomato slices in the pita. **The last thing** is add a pickle, right in the sandwich.*

- Summarization: so, finally, all in all, therefore, in closing, the last thing, at last, and so, therefore, consequently, in short, . . . .

    ***The last thing** you might do when you try to use transitions is read your piece aloud. If you hear a place where it sounds choppy or disconnected, that is probably where you need a transition.*

# Characteristics and Techniques Specific to Persuasive Writing

When young writers first try persuasion, they tend to whine, beg, make wild promises, or threaten blackmail. They need to learn about the various acceptable approaches to persuasion, the language, techniques, and arguments to use, and the supporting details that make their arguments convincing.

The following characteristics and techniques apply particularly to persuasive writing.

## Forms

Persuasive writing comes in many forms such as essays, speech writing, advertising, letters-to-the-editor, and letters to our family, friends, colleagues, potential donors or voters.

## Function

- to change a rule or policy
- to change a person's attitude
- to change a person's behavior
- to change a situation
- to ask for money
- to ask for people's votes
- to ask for a privilege
- to ask for support of a cause.

## Audience

As with most forms of exposition, a crucial aspect of persuasive writing is knowing the audience and how it will react. This will determine what kind of arguments and language to use, or avoid, and how much background information to include in the introduction. A writer must find common ground with the audience, the reader. His or her arguments must appeal to common interests and shared goals. If readers are going to change their minds, it will have to be for a good reason or for a cause they can believe in.

Therefore, an important prewriting activity for beginning persuasive writers is to identify the audience.

## Organization

Persuasive writing is characterized by a series of arguments that support an opinion or position, often in a logical order or arranged by the relative importance or strength of the arguments.

Organizationally, it is comprised of three parts: an opening statement of the author's opinion or position on an issue, a series of arguments (developed with all the kinds of supporting details writers use in any expository piece), and a final argument or conclusion drawn from the arguments. The strongest argument, saved for last, is called the clincher. It may comprise the final paragraph, but does not have to.

Many young developing writers find it useful to plan their persuasive piece in percentages of space: 10-15% for the opening, 70-75 % for the arguments, and 10-15% for the clincher and final statement. Many even fold their paper to reflect these percentages when they write a one-page persuasive piece for practice.

## Beginnings

Writers use the beginning of a persuasive piece to set forth a position or opinion. They often will include an acknowledgment of the opposition's opinion. An excellent prewriting activity for students is to list the pros and cons of an issue to determine what the opposing opinion might be. They might list the arguments that could be used against theirs, or identify their potential audience's feelings about the issue.

The beginning of a persuasive piece performs the same function as it does in any expository piece, and the same beginning hooks are appropriate. (See page 22 for Beginnings and Hooks.) There is no single *right way* to start. As long as writers accomplish the function of the introduction, they are free to be as creative as they choose. Writing is a creative art. It is thinking. It is composing.

Avoid telling students not to mix narrative with expository style. Instead, teach them how narrative can provide powerful support for their arguments. For example, a writer may start a persuasive piece with an extended case history that so vividly demonstrates his point that he need not build any further argument. He can say, essentially, "I rest my case."

Again, show your students the difference between a willy-nilly wandering in and out of narrative that represents a loss of focus, and a narrative vignette or case study that supports an idea, concept, or opinion.

*Note: Bits of expository writing are common in adult narrative fiction. Writers leave the plot line to philosophize, explain, and describe. This is actually what makes the story *adult*, what moves it beyond a children's story with a grownup plot. In *Hamlet*, Shakespeare expresses his philosophy through Polonius' advice to his son, Laertes, "Neither a borrower, nor a lender be, for loan oft loses both itself and friend." Perhaps Will had been burned by a bad loan.

Writers of children's fiction, on the other hand, purposefully avoid such expository excursions. These would interrupt the story, which is meticulously crafted to show, not tell.

## Arguments

The body of a persuasive piece may be constructed in many ways. The writer's thesis or opinion and intended audience will determine the approach.

If the readers are likely to agree, the writer will fire them to action, advancing arguments that are overwhelmingly logical and based on facts. If the readers are likely to disagree, the writer will acknowledge their position, then disarm and challenge their opposition by attacking weaknesses in their arguments. The writer will cite contrary facts, counteract myths, and point out conflicts of interests or ulterior motives.

Persuasive writing often includes a suggested compromise. A sixth-grade student wrote a brief persuasive note to a teacher that recognized the teacher's position, gave just one argument, and offered a compromise.

> *I know you have banned chewing gum in class because it can be disruptive. I would like to chew gum because it really relieves my heartburn. Couldn't I just chew it after lunch for 15 minutes? I will chew with my mouth closed.*

Young writers will find the following kinds of arguments useful in constructing their persuasive pieces.

Arguments that appeal to:

- shared values and beliefs

    *Mom, if you buy me a dog, I will learn how to take care of it. You always say how much you want me to be responsible. I will be responsible for walking, feeding, and brushing it.* (A sixth-grader in a piece to convince parent to buy him a pet.)

- common goals

    *If we had uniforms, we would look like a team.* (a third grader in a piece in favor of school uniforms.)

- common sense

    *The Renaissance program will work because it rewards kids who raise their grades. Rewarded behavior is re-peated behavior. Let's give our students a reason to excel.* (A middle-school teacher's memo to convince peers to support program.)

- benefits to the audience: financial, health, well-being (safety), and social status.

    *With a new bike I could run errands for you, like go to the store, or go to the post office. This will save you time so you can read or watch TV.* (A sixth-grader in a piece to convince parent to buy her a new bike.)

- emotion

    *A new puppy would be just the thing for our family. You have to admit you would love to cuddle with the soft, warm, and furry thing, too.* (An eighth-grader in a piece to convince parent to buy her a pet.)

- vanity

    *This magic lotion will make you look like a movie star. Imagine yourself as Queen of the Prom. This lotion will make it come true.* (A tenth-grader in a piece to convince classmates to buy an imaginary product.)

## Supporting Details for Arguments

Scientific or numerical facts, and self-evident truths are the best support for a writer's argument. Other kinds of supporting details are those described in sub-section "Characteristics and Techniques of Expository Writing."

They are:
- concrete examples
- narrative vignettes (anecdotes) that illustrate or support opinion
- authoritative quotes
- statistics
- definitions
- tables
- charts
- diagrams.

# Additional Persuasive Techniques

- **Dramatize the facts** by bringing an immediacy to them. *Just this morning, on the six o'clock news, I heard a report of this very thing — a person was evicted for displaying the American flag.*

- **Use striking statistics:** *Our school raised $6,500 dollars in pennies for the new science lab. That's over 1000 pennies per student.*

- **Use opposites for impact:** *Last year we were at the bottom of the league. This year we're at the top. Or, There's a time to reap and a time to sow.*

- **Say things repetitively but in a variety of ways.** Start several sentences with the same word or phrase, as I do in the next bulleted item.

- **Choose language that appeals to readers' emotions.** Choose language that appeals to their basic values. Choose language that triggers the right attitude or a strong emotion. (See "Word Values and Impact" in Lively Writing, page 20.)

### Transitions

Persuasive writing uses the same transitions as any expository piece (See page 26). But because persuasive writing organization is logical or based on a hierarchical order, the transition vocabulary of addition or progression is common: *First, furthermore, lastly, another, . . .*

Also, to support the persuasive technique of reiteration and emphasis, the following transitions are useful: *again, to repeat, for this reason, to emphasize, truly, in fact, as I said, to reiterate, . . .*

### Endings

The summary, commonly containing the clincher, should be short. It may reiterate the statement of opinion or main idea, draw conclusions from the facts, or refer back to the opening hook. Most of the endings used in expository writing are appropriate.

# Characteristics and Techniques Specific to Other Expository Forms

## Humorous Essay

- Function: to amuse or persuade.
- Use of literary devices: hyperbole, non sequitur, irony, onomatopoeia, personification.
- Use of the unexpected or outrageous.
- Language choice: for its emotive value, silliness, inventiveness.

## Business Letter

- Function: to inform, request, persuade.
- Special conventions of format and punctuation.
- First paragraph: Writer should get right to the object of letter. *I am writing to request, announce, inform, . . .* Or, if the letter is part of an ongoing correspondence, refer to the topic and previous contacts to bring the reader up to date. *In response to your letter of November 8th requesting, stating . . .* Or, *Confirming our phone conversation of March 12th . . .*

## Process Description

- Function: to take the reader through a series of steps to understand or accomplish something.
- Steps must be in correct order.
- Transitions of sequence and order include: *first, last, now, then, later, afterward, when, until, not until, eventually, meanwhile, immediately, soon, finally, the last thing, . . .*
- Includes definitions of new terms.
- Includes drawings to save words.

## Reviews

- Function: to give authoritative information about, or an interpretation or opinion of, a book, play, concert, event, restaurant, etc., and to influence the reader's decision whether to read, attend, or patronize it.
- Placement of factual information — who, what, where, and when — early in the piece.
- Opinion is supported with **concrete examples:** *The fish dishes are unusual. We recommend the shrimp with chocolate sauce and crab cakes oregano. Or, Shaquille O'Neal is no James Earl Jones. He delivers his lines, not much to work with in any case, in a wooden tone.*

## Directions

- Function: get reader from point A to point B, or from start to finish in a project.
- Sequence is all-important.
- Use of direction or time words should be consistent: left and right, or north, south, east, west; miles or minutes of projected travel.
- Descriptive milestones — *You will see a gas station on your right* — are helpful but should be used sparingly.
- List materials for project directions before the directions that utilize them. Example: Ingredients for cooking recipes, tools and parts for furniture or toy assembly.
- Describe and define necessary tools for projects, with illustrations if possible.
- Name the final result, destination, or the finished project.

### Information and Reports

- Function: to inform or to interpret information.
- Organization may be based on description, sequence, comparison, cause and effect, problem and solution, or combinations of these. The piece follows natural divisions specific to the organization schemes. For example, **Description:** *Baseball: players, field, rules, equipment.* Or, **Comparison:** *Zebras and horses: looks, habitats, food, habits.*

## Summary

In this primer I have introduced the major characteristics and techniques that fourth through twelfth-grade students can use to achieve lively, clear, and interesting expository writing. To present this material effectively to young writers, I have proposed combining direct instruction in these techniques with the reading aloud of well-written expository literature that illustrates their use. To complete the process, I suggested having students use these specific techniques, which I call *target skills*, in their own writing.

We need to immerse young writers aurally in the expository genre. We need to encourage them to copy the pros. By reading aloud and analyzing expository text, we give them the opportunity to develop an ear for the genre and increase the possibility they will prefer it.

## What Follows

The next section of the book contains a variety of expository samples and accompanying analyses that will get you started in your read-aloud program. Following the samples section is a source list for more read-aloud pieces. Finally, in the Appendix, you will find a compilation of expository writing advice from professional writers, and two sample expository writing workshop lessons.

# Read-Aloud Samples

## How to Use the Samples

### Selecting a Sample

1. Identify the expository writing techniques your students are studying and that you want them to hear used.
2. Browse through the analysis notes following each sample.
3. Put a page marker at each sample that highlights the skill you want your students to hear demonstrated. Several samples may illustrate the same technique, but all of them might not be appropriate for your grade level. (You will probably find examples of additional techniques you could feature that I have not included in the analysis notes. Add them to the notes or margins as you study the samples.)
4. Select the one you think best illustrates the skill you are teaching your students.

### Practicing

1. Practice reading the piece aloud. You will want to be able to read it smoothly and with feeling.

### Reading the Sample Aloud

1. Tell your students what form the piece takes: review, essay, persuasion, informational, etc.
2. Remind your students of the expository writing technique they have been studying. Write it on the board. Example: The use of a narrative vignette to illustrate a point. Or, lively writing with strong verbs or literary devices.
3. Read the sample through without stopping for discussion.

## Rereading and Analyzing the Sample

1. Now ask your student to listen specifically for the technique as you **reread** the selection.
2. Ask them to jot down a few words to identify the place where they heard the author use the technique.
3. Reread the part where the students identified the targeted technique. Discuss how the author used the technique.

## After the Reading

1. Suggest to your young writers that they copy the pros — try out this skill in their next expository piece.
2. Invite students to read parts of their own writing aloud to the class where they have used the same technique.
3. Read other samples from this book, and ones you have found elsewhere, that demonstrate the use of the expository technique under study.
4. Invite students to find samples in their reading that demonstrate this skill. Provide time for them to read these samples to the class.

# Cobwebs To Crosshairs!

## by
## Carol Ann Moorhead

Cobwebs in your telescope? Could be — no matter how often you dust!

Imbedded in the lenses of many telescopes are two strands of spider silk. Don't think you can see them? Think again. If you can see the crosshairs in your telescopes, you can see the "cobwebs."

Crosshairs haven't always been made of spider silk. Early astronomers peered past platinum wires and through heavily ruled glass to view and chart the night skies. But by the 1900s, telescope manufacturers were using spider silk for crosshairs.

It's easy to see why. Spider silk is less expensive, easier to stretch into a straight line, and more resistant to extreme temperatures than platinum. It is also much finer. The average strand of spider silk is 1/1,970 of a centimeter wide — about 20 times finer than a human hair!

Now, spider-silk crosshairs are spinning out of existence. According to Alan Hale, president of Celestron International (a telescope maker), spider silk is being phased out in favor of less costly but thicker copper wire. At 1/276 of a centimeter wide, the new copper strands are only 3 times finer than a human hair.

Cobwebs in you next telescope? Not likely — unless you leave the cap off the lens! ☆

# Informational Expository

## (Magazine article)

"**Cobwebs to Crosshairs**," by Carol Ann Moorhead, appeared in the February 1996 issue of the children's science magazine," *Odyssey*." She is the author of *Wild Horses* (Roberts Rinehart, 1994) and author/illustrator of *Colorado's Backyard Wildlife* (Roberts Rinehart, 1992).

I love the way the author begins and ends this piece. She echoes the lead in the ending. Also, I have to admit it; I'm partial to science writing.

## Writing features to listen for

**FUNCTION**   To inform and explain.

**ORGANIZATION**   Natural division of the topic into components: Pre-spider silk use, spider silk, post-spider silk. Or, history, description of crosshairs, modern crosshairs.

### BEGINNING

**Hook:** Question and exclamation: *Cobwebs in your telescope? Could be — no matter how often you dust!*  Makes reader curious to find out more.

**Introduction:** Author reveals suprising fact: There's spider silk in a telescope lens. *Imbedded in the lenses of many telescopes are two strands of spider silk. Don't think you can see them? Think again. If you can see the* **crosshairs** *in your telescopes, you can see the* **"cobwebs."**

### SUPPORTING DETAILS

**Historical material:** *Early astronomers peered past platinum wires and through heavily ruled glass to view and chart the night skies.*

**Numbers:** *The average strand of spider silk is 1/1,970 of a centimeter wide — about 20 times finer than a human hair!*

**Descriptive details:** *Spider silk is less expensive, easier to stretch into a straight line, and more resistant to extreme temperatures than platinum. It is also much finer.*

➡

**Authoritative quote:** *According to Alan Hale, president of Celestron International (a telescope maker), spider silk is being phased out in favor of less costly but thicker copper wire.*

**Comparisons:** *Spider silk is less expensive, easier to stretch; 20 times finer than a human hair; ...less costly but thicker copper wire.*

## LIVELY WRITING

**Talks directly to the reader:** Invites reader to think back to an experience with a telescope.

**People-oriented:** Writer uses *you, your,* and names people: early astronomers, *Alan Hale, president of Celestron International (a telescope maker),*

**Play on words:** *Now, spider-silk crosshairs are spinning out of existence.* (Spiders spin webs.)

**Alliteration:** *peered past platinum, stretch into a straight, phased out in favor.*

**The writer has fun:** She tricks us at the start, using the words "*cobwebs*" to lead us to the imagery of old, dusty, long unused. Then, she sets us straight: we're talking spider web silk. At the end she pulls us back to our first dusty, cobwebby image. *Cobwebs in your next telescope? Not likely — unless you leave the cap off the lens!*

**ENDING** The ending reiterates the hook with a variation based on opposite. The hook: *Cobwebs in your telescope? <u>Could be</u>.* The end: *Cobwebs in your next telescope? <u>Not likely</u>.* ✰

# Camp Fish Is in a Class by Itself:

## Give kids the time of their lives, and a gift to be treasured for a lifetime.

Deep in the backwoods of Minnesota's north country, there's a secluded place where kids wake at the crack of dawn, stay busy learning all day, and go to sleep wishing the day had never ended.

That's Camp Fish.

Camp Fish is more than just a camp. It's an education and an experience. Camp Fish not only teaches kids how to fish, but also instills a love and appreciation for the outdoors. At Camp Fish kids catch something to prize forever. As Steve Lund, Camp Director says, "Many kids leave here feeling it's been the greatest experience of their lives. It gives them a sense of self-worth and self-respect, and puts the rest of the world in perspective."

The Camp Fish program, designed by the top experts in the fishing world, features a four-year curriculum for kids 10 to 16. Beginners spend six days in camp each summer and take part in instruction ranging from boating and water safety, to basic freshwater ecology and conservation. By the time a young angler completes the four-year program, he or she has learned advanced boat handling and outdoor skills, as well as how to locate and catch bass, walleye, northern pike, muskies, trout, and panfish. And let's not forget making their own lures and rods, and baitcasting and flycasting equipment; not to mention the proper use of electronic equipment, and how to fillet fish and cook them, too. The four-year

➥

program culminates in a fly-in fishing trip to Canadian waters.

Kids love it! Over 70% of all youngsters who attend Camp Fish return for more advanced training. This fact alone tell the Camp Fish story.

Camp Fish counselors and instructors are all well trained, totally committed professionals, completely prepared to supervise the program. The program boasts six aquatic biologists, and water safety, physical education, and conservation instructors. They're all patient and friendly, and just happen to be expert anglers, too.

A staff of 30 ensures a student-to-counselor ratio of about 3-1. You can't beat that in this day of increasing class sizes. It's a personal touch that makes all the difference.

The most important aspect of Camp Fish is that everyone can participate. Not just big kids, fast kids, rich kids, or brilliant kids, but all sorts of kids, with all sorts of talents, and from all sorts of backgrounds. Camp Fish is for kids who love fishing.

Fishing is one tie that binds parents, grandparents, or interested adults to children. In a world of education, gender, race, age, religious, and a dozen other so called "gaps," fishing still bridges all barriers.

A week of fishing in the Minnesota north woods. Hearty meals in a rustic lodge. New friends. Reliving it all around a crackling campfire. That's Camp Fish. ☆

# Persuasive Writing

## ( Advertisement )

**"Camp Fish Is in a Class by Itself,"** is an advertisement that appears in each issue of "The In-Fisherman Magazine". The editor, Doug Stange, granted me permission to reprint it.

I selected this piece because it contains several kinds of arguments students can use in their persuasive writing. The writer uses the important persuasive technique of repetition. The language is simple, with few big words, yet the piece is rich in descriptive details, emotive and positive words, and alliteration. Doesn't it make you want to go fishing?

### Writing features to listen for

**FUNCTION**  To persuade. The ad's goal is to get the reader to sign up (or sign their kids up) for Camp Fish's summer program.

**ORGANIZATION**  Standard persuasive format: Opinion, arguments, clincher. The writer presents compelling arguments to convince the reader it is *the* camp to attend.

**BEGINNING**
  **Hook:** How can it be so good that kids wish each day had never ended? Wow! *Deep in the backwoods of Minnesota's north country, there's a secluded place where kids wake at the crack of dawn, stay busy learning all day, and go to sleep wishing the day had never ended.*

  **Introduction:** Setting and background information about the camp: *Camp Fish is more than just a camp. It's an education and an experience. Camp Fish not only teaches kids how to fish, but also instills a love and appreciation for the outdoors. At Camp Fish kids catch something to prize forever.*

**ARGUMENTS**
  **Appeal to common values:**
  • Nature education: *love and appreciation of outdoors*
  • Fairness: It's for everyone.

➡

- Socialization: *Fishing is one tie that binds parents, grand-parents, or interested adults to children. In a world of education, gender, race, age, religious, and a dozen other so called "gaps," fishing still bridges all barriers.*

**Appeal to aesthetics:** *secluded woods, Canadian waters, rustic lodge.*

**Benefits to audience:**
- Education: *boating and water safety; basic freshwater ecology and conservation; advanced boat handling and outdoor skills; how to locate and catch bass, walleye . . . ; making their own lures and rods, and baitcasting and flycasting equipment; the proper use of electronic equip-ment; how to fillet fish and cook them. Counselors are qualified and committed.*
- Personal attention: Small class size with personal touch.

## SUPPORTING DETAILS

**Descriptive details:** *Deep in the backwoods of Minnesota's north country, there's a secluded place where kids wake at the crack of dawn; fishing in the Minnesota north woods; Hearty meals in a rustic lodge; New friends; Reliving it all around a crackling campfire.*

**Proofs:** *Camp Fish is more that just a camp. Proof: Camp Fish not only teaches kids how to fish, but also instills a love and appreciation for the outdoors; Kids love it! Proof: Over 70% of all youngsters who attend Camp Fish return for more advanced training.*

**Numbers/statistics:** *A staff of 30 ensures a student-to-counselor ratio of about 3-1; Over 70% of all youngsters...*

**Authoritative quote:** *As Steve Lund, Camp Director says, "Many kids leave here feeling it's been the greatest experience of their lives. It gives them a sense of self-worth and self-respect, and puts the rest of the world in perspective."*

## LIVELY WRITING

**People-oriented:** *Kids love it; youngsters; aquatic biologists; instructors; Let's not forget; parents, grandparents.*

**Sentence and Paragraph Variation:** Sentences range from three words to thirty-six. Paragraphs range from one sentence to five; The use of *And* to start a sentence; Incomplete

➡

sentences for effect in the last paragraph. Sentences contain phrases that answer: where, when, how, which kind, why.

**Repetition:** *Camp Fish* (repeated 10 times)

**Language:** Words chosen for their connotative and emotive value; *secluded, education, experience, instill a love and appreciation, personal touch, friendly, treasure for a lifetime, expert anglers, rustic lodge, crackling campfire.*

**Contractions:** Create informal tone: *they're, there's, that's, let's.*

**Strong verbs:** *Camp Fish instills, program boasts, program features, a young angler completes, program culminates, staff ensures, counselors are prepared, everyone can participate.*

**Literary devices: alliteration;** *kids catch, sense of self-worth, features a four year, fillet fish, fly-in fishing trip, bridges all barriers, crackling campfire.*

**Idioms or expressions:** *crack of dawn, the tie that binds.*

**TRANSITIONS** additive: *. . . not only . . . . . but also; And let's not forget; Not to mention, too.*

**ENDING**

**Reiteration of benefits:** Use of incomplete sentences to name the benefits of attending Camp Fish. *A week of fishing in the Minnesota north woods. Hearty meals in a rustic lodge. New friends. Reliving it all around a crackling campfire. That's Camp Fish.*

**Repeat of the phrase in the introduction:** *That's Camp Fish.* ☆

# A Movie So Dull It's Scary

## by
## David Grimes

More and more, the motto of the American movie industry seems to be: If you liked the comic book, you'll love the movie. While this is not necessarily a bad thing, it would be nice if movie makers could at least choose a decent comic book to film.

I'm not saying that "Casper, The Friendly Ghost" was a bad comic book; all I'm saying is that the main character was — and I'm trying to be gentle here — a wimp.

Correct me if I'm wrong, but it seems to me that the whole point of being a ghost is to scare the bejeebers out of people. You know: move furniture around, cause rooms to go suddenly cold, rattle chains, that sort of stuff.

Ghosts are supposed to haunt. It's in their job description. If you buy a haunted house, you expect it to come with ghosts. Scary ghosts, not ghosts that offer you milk and cookies and tell you to have a nice day.

Casper gave real ghosts a bad name. He was about as threatening as a bowl of chicken noodle soup. You were in more danger folding laundry.

Casper didn't want to scare people; he wanted people to like him. Unfortunately for Casper, people didn't understand that he was a friendly ghost and had the bejeebers scared out of them anyway.

Which is another annoying thing about the comic book. These people, they'd see Casper

➡

and the hair would stand up on their heads and their eyes would bug out and ...well, you just wanted to slap 'em is what you wanted to do.

Then grab them by the shoulders and shake them hard while screaming, "You fools! Can't you see that this pathetic little dweeb means you no harm? See? Big, round head? Soft, compassionate eyes? Lopsided grin? There are some haircuts out there that are more menacing! This isn't Wesley Snipes we're talking about here, folks; it's a pudgy little ghost who's so kind that he'd hug a skunk just to make a friend."

You've got to wonder what kind of message this sends out to kids. Are we telling them that you can't be kind and gentle unless you are also dull as toast?

So just don't do a "Casper" movie, you comic book loving directors, because Casper basically has the personality of tapioca pudding. ☆

# Humorous Essay
## (Humor newspaper column)

**"A Movie So Dull It's Scary,"** by David Grimes, humor columnist, appeared in the *Sarasota Herald Tribune* on May 30, 1995.

Humor challenges a writer like no other genre. The writer can employ none of the comedic tools the stand-up comic uses; body language and movements, facial expression, the pause, the audience reaction. Only words.

In this piece, the writer pretends to be serious about the movie industry's current obsession with comic book characters for movie heroes. In the guise of a persuasive essay, he applies the tools of his trade: hyperbole, outrageous or unexpected analogies, funny words and expressions, looking at things from a different angle, treating a frivolous topic with exaggerated seriousness, tongue-in-cheek observations, irony, and such. The result is a hilarious piece.

## Writing features to listen for

**FUNCTION**  To amuse. The writer does it in the guise of a persuasive essay.

**ORGANIZATION**  Standard persuasive form: opinion statement, followed by a series of arguments, conclusion including the clincher.

**BEGINNING**
   **Hook:** Alliteration: *More and more, the motto of the American movie industry seems to be . . .*
   **Introduction:** David Grimes states his opinion; making a movie about Casper, the comic character, is a big mistake . . . . *it would be nice if movie makers could at least choose a decent comic book to film.* Then he sets out to convince us with a series of arguments.

➡

## ARGUMENTS

**Appeal to common sense:** *Correct me if I'm wrong, but it seems to me that the whole point of being a ghost is to scare the bejeebers out of people; If you buy a haunted house, you expect it to come with ghosts; Ghosts are supposed to haunt; Ghosts are supposed to be scary; Casper gives ghosts a bad name.*

## SUPPORTING DETAILS

**Definition:** *A ghost is supposed to haunt, move furniture around, cause rooms to go suddenly cold, rattle chains, that sort of stuff.*

**Comparison:** *Scary ghosts, not ghosts that offer you milk and cookies and tell you to have a nice day; as threatening as a bowl of chicken soup; basically the personality of tapioca pudding; You were in more danger folding laundry; This isn't Wesley Snipes we're talking about here, folks; So kind that he'd hug a skunk just to make a friend.*

**Descriptive details:** *big round head, soft compassionate eyes, lopsided grin, pudgy little ghost.*

**Cites contrary facts:** *He is too friendly; he is kind; he is as threatening as a bowl of chicken soup.*

## LIVELY, HUMOROUS WRITING

**Talks directly to reader:** uses *I, you, me*

**Word choice and contractions:** Create informal tone; *wimp, folks, bejeepers, pudgy, pathetic little dweeb, kids; 'em, didn't, I'm, who's, he'd, don't, you've, isn't, it's, they'd, can't.*

**Tongue-in-cheek** (pseudo-serious, only kidding):

- *. . . all I'm saying is that the main character was — and I'm trying to be gentle here — a wimp.*
- *You've got to wonder what kind of message this sends out to kids. Are we telling them that you can't be kind and gentle unless you are also dull as toast?*
- *Ghosts are supposed to haunt. It's in their job description*
- *There are some haircuts out there that are more menacing!*

➤

**Literary devices:**

> **Simile:** *as threatening as a bowl of chicken soup*
> *the personality of tapioca pudding*
> *so kind he'd hug a skunk to make a friend*
> *as dull as toast*

> **Alliteration:** *More and more, the motto; not necessarily; haunted house; more menacing; shoulders and shake; can't be kind; he'd hug.*

> **Hyperbole:** *You were in more danger folding laundry.*

> **Anadiplosis:** (The repetition of a word ending one sentence or phrase, at the beginning of the next phrase or sentence.) *. . . you want it to come with* **ghosts. Scary ghosts,** *not ghosts that offer you . . .*

**TRANSITIONS** Notice the writer uses only one additive transition phrase: *Which is another annoying thing . . .* The reader expects a series of arguments in a persuasive essay and does not have to be hit over the head with, *Next, Furthermore, Secondly,* and so forth.

**ENDING** The writer signals the summary paragraph with the word, *So.* It circles back to the writer's original assertion that the movie makers shouldn't pick the comic book Casper as the basis for a new movie. It contains the clincher, Casper has no personality. *So, just don't do a "Casper" movie, you comic-book-loving directors, because Casper basically has the personality of tapioca pudding.* ☆

# Chocolate

**by**
**George S. Fichter**

Chocolate! Just thinking about a piece of sweet chocolate candy or a cup of foamy hot chocolate can make your mouth water.

Today almost anyone can buy chocolate. But it wasn't always that way. Until the 1500s, chocolate was a secret known only to the people of Central and South America.

In 1519 the Spanish explorer Hernán Cortés reported that the Aztecs in Mexico drank amazing amounts of something they called *chocllatl* (show-co-LAH-tul). This watery, bitter drink was made from mysterious and prized beans from a tree they called *kakahuatl* (ka-ka-joo-AH-tul).

Montezuma, the Aztec king, drank 50 golden goblets of the drink every day. Montezuma's palace staff drank 2000 pitchers of it! Cortes figured that if an Aztec king liked *chocolatl*, a Spanish king would too. So he took some beans back to Europe as one of the fabulous treasures of America.

The Spanish royalty called their new drink chocolate (cho-co-LAH-tay). They sweetened it with sugar or honey and flavored it with cinnamon. The supply of beans was limited and they didn't want to share them with anyone. They kept their chocolate a secret so that, for many years, very few people in Europe knew about chocolate.

The great taste of chocolate reached North America in 1765. That's when the first

➡

chocolate factory opened in New England. Even Thomas Jefferson got the chocolate habit. He and many others believed that chocolate was good for their health.

Over the years, *kakahuatl* trees became known as cacao (cah-COW) trees. And today they're grown in tropical countries around the world. If you saw a cacao tree, the first things you'd notice would be its football-shaped bean pods. The pods grow right out from the tree's trunks and branches.

Inside each of the pods is gooey, white, sweet-tasting pulp. When people harvest the pods, they often eat some of the pulp as a treat while they work. Inside the pulp are 30 to 40 purplish cacao beans. If you chewed on a bean right out of the pod, it would be so bitter that you'd spit it out.

After the pods are picked, the pulp and beans are taken out. The beans are then left to soak in the pulp for three to seven days. During that time, chemicals inside the beans change. The pulp also begins to rot and drain away. When the beans start smelling like chocolate, they are dried in the sun. Finally, they are shipped to chocolate-making factories all over the world.

At chocolate factories, first the beans are roasted, then shattered and shaken, tumbled over and over again, and ground up into tiny bits. These bits are then melted down into a thick paste called chocolate *liquor.* (This liquor has no alcohol in it.)

Chocolate liquor is the "secret ingredient" in all kinds of chocolate products. Pure chocolate liquor is hardened and sold as

➡

unsweetened baking chocolate. Semisweet chocolate has enough sugar added to make it taste good. Sweet chocolate candy has even more sugar in it. Milk chocolate is made by adding milk.

Chocolate is eaten by millions of people around the world, but very few of them know chocolate's history. If they did, they'd all be glad that chocolate was a secret nobody could keep! ☆

# Informational and Process Description

## (Magazine article)

"**Chocolate**," by George S. Fichter, is reprinted from the February 1996 issue of *Ranger Rick* magazine, with the permission of the publisher, the National Wildlife Federation. Copyright 1996 by the National Wildlife Federation.

I selected this piece one day when I was hungry. It combines historical background and process description. After the introduction, the first half the article is written in the past tense, narrative style, chronicling the history of chocolate. The second half describes the chocolate-making process, expository style, and is in the present tense. The piece contains a nice variety of process transition words.

Note the prevalence of two-sentence paragraphs. Short paragraphs are typical of informational magazine articles. The reader appreciates small bites of information; the printed page has an open, light, inviting, and unintimidating look. There is no rule that a paragraph has to have a certain number of sentences.

### Writing features to listen for

**FUNCTION**  To inform and explain.

**ORGANIZATION**  Two part: Narrative: chronological order. Process description: sequence of steps.

**BEGINNING**
   **Hook:** Exclamation and imagery: *Chocolate! Just thinking about a piece of sweet chocolate candy or a cup of foamy hot chocolate can make your mouth water.*
   **Introduction:** Sets up the theme: *Today almost anyone can buy chocolate. But it wasn't always that way. Until the 1500s, chocolate was a secret known only to the people of Central and South America.* (see ENDING).

**SUPPORTING DETAILS**
   **Dates:** *1500s, 1519, 1765*

➡

**Definitions:** *choclatl, a watery, bitter drink made from beans; chocolate liquor, a thick paste; semisweet chocolate has more sugar added; mild chocolate has added milk.*

**Numbers:** *2,000 pitchers, 50 goblets, 30-40 purplish cacao beans.*

**Descriptive details:** *football-shaped bean pods, purplish beans, sweet-tasting pulp, begins to rot and drain, melted down to a thick paste.*

**Comparisons:** *so bitter you would spit it out.*

## LIVELY WRITING

**People-oriented:** *King Montezuma, Aztecs, Hernán Cortés, Spanish royalty, Thomas Jefferson.*

**Talks directly to reader:** *If you saw a cacao tree, the first thing you'd notice; If you chewed on a bean right out of the pod, it would be so bitter you'd spit it out.*

**Literary devices: alliteration;** *amazing amounts, golden goblets, beans back, tree trunks, people harvest the pods, pods are picked, shattered and shaken.*

**Short paragraphs:** Makes the article fast-moving.

**TRANSITIONS** Process transition words: *When, After, During that time, First, Finally.*

## SPECIAL NOTE

**Parallel construction:** Series of sentences in the next to last paragraph all start with the name of a chocolate and then explain what it is.

**ENDING** Echos the content and words of the Introduction, i.e., today's universality of chocolate, yesterday's secret. Start: *Today almost anyone can buy chocolate.* Ending: *Chocolate is eaten by millions* . . . Start: *Until the 1500s, chocolate was a secret* . . . Ending: *they'd all be glad that chocolate was a secret nobody could keep.* ✰

# Another Rabbit

### by
### Krista Kluding

Dear Mom and Dad,

I need another rabbit. I know you don't want me to get another rabbit, but listen to my facts. I'm sure by the end of my letter I will have convinced you.

I could breed a new rabbit with the one I already have. I know you are saying, "NO" in your head, but I could sell the bunnies and make money. Wouldn't it also be fun to hold those cute little balls of fur?

I would also take care of her. As you know, I take care of the rabbit I have. I would spend time with them and I would let them out a lot. You always say taking care of the rabbit is making me more responsible.

Now, I know you are both saying, "Absolutely not, it costs too much money." But I would pay for her and the food, the supplies, and the whole nine yards. Of course, you might have to raise my allowance.

I could enter her in the Fair. Isn't that brilliant? She could win awards and I would get even more involved with 4-H. And that's good, isn't it?

My last thing to say, especially to you, Dad, is it would save us money if we were ever starving. Think of all the possibilities there would be: Rabbit stew, roasted rabbit, rabbit à la mode, rabbit pie, boiled rabbit, baked rabbit, stuffed rabbit, and even rabbit pot pie. I'm just kidding, but it crossed my mind.

➡

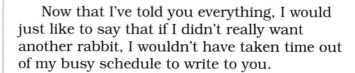

Now that I've told you everything, I would just like to say that if I didn't really want another rabbit, I wouldn't have taken time out of my busy schedule to write to you.

Yours truly,
Krista ☆

# Persuasive Essay

## (Student paper)

**"Another Rabbit,"** was written by Krista Kluding, a sixth-grade student, in response to a class assignment.

Young writers enjoy hearing other students' writing. This author has mastered some of the skills of a humor writer: saying the outrageous and unexpected, using hyperbole, and using idiomatic expressions in a funny way. She has combined these skills with those she has learned about the persuasive essay in one funny piece.

## Writing features to listen for

**FUNCTION**  To persuade and amuse.

**ORGANIZATION**  Standard persuasive form: opinion statement, a series of arguments, with the strongest one (the clincher) saved for last.
   **Strategy:** The writer uses humor to disarm the opposition (her parents).

**BEGINNING**  Statement of purpose, acknowledgment of opposition's stand, invitation to read further.

**ARGUMENTS**  Anticipates parents' counter-arguments and addresses each one.
   **Appeal to emotion:** *Wouldn't it be fun to hold the cute little balls of fur?*
   **Appeal to common values:** *I would be responsible, taking care of the rabbit; I would earn money.*
   **Benefits to audience:** *I would get more involved in 4-H; If we were ever starving, we could eat it.*

## LIVELY, HUMOROUS WRITING
   **Humor:** Use of the outrageous and unexpected: *Of course you might have to raise my allowance; Isn't that brilliant?; We can eat rabbits;  I wouldn't have taken time out of my busy schedule.*
   **Hyperbole:** The extended list of rabbit dishes.

➡

**Language:** Words chosen for emotive value; *cute little balls of fur, the whole nine yards.*

**COPY THE PROS** The writer imitates the screen writers of *Forrest Gump.* Her list of rabbit dishes mimics the movie-character Bubba's list of shrimp dishes.

**ENDING** Restatement of the author's request, parroting a grownup expression in a facetious way, to demonstrate the depth of her feeling: *I wouldn't have taken time out of my busy schedule.* ☆

# Don't Be Afraid to Fall

### by
### Harry J. Gray

You've failed many times,
although you may not
remember.
You fell down
the first time
you tried to walk.
You almost drowned
the first time
you tried to
swim, didn't you?
Did you hit the
ball the first time
you swung a bat?
Heavy hitters,
the ones who hit the most home runs,
also strike
out a lot.
English novelist
John Creasey got
752 rejection slips
before he published
564 books.
Babe Ruth struck out
1,330 times,
but he also hit 714 home runs.
Don't worry about failure.
Worry about the
chances you miss
when you don't
even try. ☆

# Persuasive Essay

**"Don't Be Afraid to Fall,"** is one of a series of inspirational essays by Harry J. Gray, former Chairman and CEO of United Technologies, that appeared in the *Wall Street Journal* in the 1980s. It is reproduced here in its original format and reprinted with the permission of United Technologies Corporation.

One of my son's teachers told him that over 80% of what you learn in life you learn by trial and error. I agree, and hope this piece will persuade your students of it. I also hope they will try out some of the highlighted expository techniques the piece demonstrates.

## Writing features to listen for

**FUNCTION** To persuade. To convince the reader to strive to accomplish, without fearing failure or the possibility of it.

**ORGANIZATION** Persuasive form with opinion statement (in the title), arguments, and conclusion.

**ARGUMENTS**
  **Appeals to common sense:** Failure is a normal part of life: *You've failed many times; Heavy hitters, the ones who hit the most home runs, also strike out a lot.*

**SUPPORTING DETAILS**
  **Specific, concrete examples:** *You fell the first time you walked; almost drowned; struck out first time;* Famous achievers have failed: *John Creasey got 752 rejection slips, Babe Ruth struck out 1,330 times.*
  **Numbers or statistics:** *752 rejection slips, struck out 1,330 times.*

**LIVELY WRITING**
  **Talks directly to reader:** Points to readers' experiences — reader can say, "Yes, that's me."
  **Reiterates:** Repeats phrases: *the first time, worry.*
  **Alliteration:** *heavy hitter, hit the most homeruns*
  **Short, easy-to-follow sentences.**

**ENDING** Restatement of the opinion, with additional advice. ☆

# Illustrating a Book is Kind of Like This

### by
### Frank Remkiewicz

Most of the books I illustrate are picture books. They usually have 32 pages with a picture on almost every one. So, the first thing I do is break up the writer's manuscript into small sections that will each become a picture page. I do this sectioning with light pencil marks on the manuscript.

I make sure that each bit of action or adventure has its own picture. Parts of the story that are scary or funny deserve a full page picture. Parts that are quiet or sad come in second but often get pictures too. Sometimes authors go overboard with dialogue that has no action to illustrate. I leave these parts alone to go on a words-only page.

Next, I make a paper mock up — a dummy — of the book, sketching in all the pictures and leaving room for the words. I make the sketches simple and easy to change. Just as the writer revises the story until it is just right, I revise my pictures until they are just right. Sometimes a scene needs to be larger or smaller, or a character needs to be seen from a different point-of-view, perhaps from a bird's-eye view or from a bug's-eye view.

When I am happy with the way the pictures look and how they help the story flow from start to finish, I begin the final artwork. I place a sheet of art paper over a sketched page of the dummy. I place them on top of a light

➡

box, which allows me to see my rough sketch through the thick art paper. I carefully trace over each sketched page with pencil, pen, or non-bleeding marker.

Then I go into a kind of mass production. I have to set up my palette, brushes, water bucket, and a pencil sharpener. Using water-color, colored pencils, and markers, I color all the components that appear over and over in the book. Sometimes I use gouache, (pro-nounced gwash) which is an expensive kind of poster paint that comes in tubes. I skip from page to page, painting all the skin, carpeting, wallpaper, grass, buildings, and such. Then I finish each of the sketches off with the details.

It takes me a couple of months or more to paint all 32 pictures that make up an average picture book. When I'm finished I cover each painting with a piece of paper called a *flap*, to protect it from scratches or stains or finger-prints. Next, they all go into a flat box or manila envelope, and I mail them to the com-pany that will publish the book.

The editors of the publishing company check to see if I forgot any little details. (Some-times I do, and they send a painting back for me to add a detail.) When they are satisfied with the pictures and the text, they send everything on to a printer who prints the pages of the book. The printer sends the printed pages to the bindery where they are glued and sewn together and a cardboard cover attached. Soon after, the book shows up in your school, a bookstore, or the public library. And I take a nap. Whew! ☆

# Process Description

**"Illustrating a Book Is Kind of Like This,"** by Frank Remkiewicz, was written expressly for this book. Remkiewicz is a children's book illustrator and author. His illustrated works include The *Froggy* series by Jonathan London, the *Horrible Harry* series by Suzy Kline, and *The Joy Boys*, by Betsy Byars. He wrote and illustrated *Fiona Raps It Up*.

Here is a process description especially selected for the student illustrators in your writing workshop, but of interest to all. The author uses lots of specific examples and gives the reasons for each thing he does.

## Writing features to listen for

**FUNCTION**  To describe a process.

**ORGANIZATION**  Sequence of steps from start to finish.

**TRANSITIONS**  Illustrate the sequence and indicate how long a step takes: *So, the first thing I do . . . , Next . . . , When I am happy . . . , Then I go into . . . , Then I finish . . . , It takes me a couple of months . . . , When I am finished . . . , Soon, the book . . .*

**SUPPORTING DETAILS**
   **Definitions:**  *picture books. They usually have 32 pages with a picture on almost every one.; a paper mock up — a dummy — of the book; Sometimes I use gouache, (pronounced gwash) which is an expensive kind of poster paint that comes in tubes.; I cover each painting with a piece of paper called a flap, to protect it from scratches or stains or fingerprints.*

   **Descriptive details:**  *I do this sectioning with light pencil marks on the manuscript.; Parts of the story that are scary or funny; Parts that are quiet or sad come in second; a light box, which allows me to see my rough sketch through the thick art paper; a flat box or manila envelope; the printed pages are glued and sewn together and a cardboard cover attached.*

   **Numbers:**  *32 pages, a couple of months or more.*

   **Comparisons:**  *a scene needs to be larger or smaller; character needs to be seen from a different point-of-view, perhaps from a bird's-eye view or from a bug's-eye view.*

➡

**Specific examples:** *I set up my palette, brushes, water bucket, and a pencil sharpener.; Using watercolor, colored pencils, and markers; painting all the skin, carpeting, wallpaper, grass, buildings, and such.*

## LIVELY WRITING

**Talks directly to the readers:** Uses the words *I, you, me.*

**Analogy:** *Just as the writer revises the story until it is just right, I revise my pictures until they are just right.*

**Active verbs:** *I break up, I make sure, parts of the story deserve, authors go overboard, I do this sectioning, I revise, I place, I carefully trace, I skip, I cover, I mail them, editors check, they send, book shows up.*

**ENDING** Tells, humorously, how he feels after process is complete: *And I take a nap. Whew!* Reader learns that illustrating a book is hard work. ☆

# It's What You Do — Not When You Do It

### by
### Harry J. Gray

Ted Williams, at age 42,
slammed a home run
in his last official
time at bat.
Mickey Mantle, age 20,
hit 23 home runs
his first full year
in the major leagues.
Golda Meir was 71 when
she became Prime Minister
of Israel.
William Pitt II was 24
when he became
Prime Minister of
Great Britain.
George Bernard Shaw was 94
when one of his plays
was first produced.
Mozart was just 7
when his first composition
was published.
Now, how about this?
Benjamin Franklin
was a newspaper columnist
at 16,
and a framer of The United
States Constitution
when he was 81.
You're never too young
or too old,
if you've got talent.
Let's recognize
that age has little to do
with ability. ☆

# Persuasive Essay

**"It's What You Do — Not When You Do It,"** is one of a series of inspirational essays by Harry J. Gray, Chairman and CEO of United Technologies, that appeared in the *Wall Street Journal* in the 1980s. It is reproduced here in its original format and reprinted with the permission of United Technologies Corporation.

I like this piece especially for its inspirational message, but also because it perfectly demonstrates how a writer can build his case simply by providing lots of examples. By the time the writer expresses his opinion, the reader has been convinced by the sheer weight of the evidence.

## Writing features to listen for

**FUNCTION**  To persuade.

**ORGANIZATION**  Standard persuasive form: state opinion, (in the title) present arguments supported by details, reiterate opinion. To support his opinion, the writer uses a form of argument (inductive reasoning) that goes from the specific to the general. The reader has to read all the specific examples to accept the general conclusion at the end. The writer's arguments are presented as **a list.**

**BEGINNING**
> **Hook:** Name of a famous person: *Ted Williams*
>
> **No introduction** to the topic in the text. The title performs that function.

**PERSUASIVE TECHNIQUE**
> **Facts:** a list of historical facts, which no one can dispute.
>
> **Contrast:** *old, young*

**LIVELY WRITING**
> **People-oriented: Proper nouns:** people are named.
>
> **Talks directly to reader:** *you, Let's*

**ADDITIONAL TECHNIQUES**
> **Sentences:** Short, easy to follow.

➡

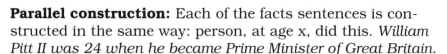

**Parallel construction:** Each of the facts sentences is constructed in the same way: person, at age x, did this. *William Pitt II was 24 when he became Prime Minister of Great Britain.*

**Transition:** *Now, how about this?* signals a new form of presentation for Ben Franklin's accomplishments; telling what he did when he was young and what he did when he was old, which is the clincher.

**ENDING**  Restates the title opinion: *Let's recognize that age has little to do with ability.* After all the examples, the reader is likely to accept the writer's opinion and conclusion.  ☆

# Myths of the Milky Way

## by
## Jim O'Leary

Early humans gazed in awe at the mysterious ribbon of light we now call the Milky Way, wondering what it was, where it went, and what it was made of. Over time, cultures from around the world have given us many fanciful stories about our home galaxy.

From the ancient Romans came the name "Milky Way," or in Latin, "Via Lactea." The Greeks called it "Kiklos Galaxias," or the Milky Circle, the mother's milk of the Goddess Juno spilled across the heavens as she fed the infant Hercules.

Many civilizations saw the Milky Way as a path, or river, twisting through the heavens. The Tartars of central Russia considered it to be a thief's path marked by stolen straw he had dropped. Some Muslims envisioned pilgrims on their way to Mecca, the holiest city of Islam, in Saudi Arabia, in the light of the Milky Way. Another legend has St. James appearing to the ruler Charlemagne, King of the Franks (768-814), showing him the way to Spain and the saint's tomb.

Some Eskimos, or Inuits, of North America picture it as a path of glowing ashes guiding travelers back home, while other see it as the path of the Great Raven. In Estonia and Lapland, it was believed to be the route of migrating birds, and some Finns saw it as a path of wild geese.

The Chinese pictured a great heavenly river, leading to an abyss, where the mother of

➡

the sun and the mother of the moon bathed their children before returning them to the sky.

Many cultures regarded the Milky Way as the path for souls departing for the afterlife. North American Indians thought it marked the way for ghosts, leading to the "land of the hereafter." Other stories link the Milky Way to the daytime sky, where it and the rainbow are considered as two passageways uniting heaven and Earth.

Australian aborigines have so many stars in their dark skies that the seemingly empty patches scattered through the Milky Way are unique. In them, they see a giant emu (an ostrichlike-bird) stretching across the sky.

Perhaps the most creative Milky Way legend comes from the Kalahari bushmen, of southern Africa. To them, the mysterious cloud is the backbone of night, holding together and supporting the great vault of the sky.

Next time you are surrounded by darkness on a clear night, look up at the Milky Way and imagine you don't know what it really is. What does it look like to you? What would you think of it if you lived long ago? ☆

# Informational Expository

## (Magazine article)

**"Myths of the Milky Way,"** by Jim O'Leary is from "ODYSSEY," May 1995 issue: "Galaxies: Building Blocks of the Universe," © 1995, Cobblestone Publishing, Inc., 7 School St., Peterborough, NH 03458. Reprinted by permission of the publisher.

I selected this piece for the interesting way in which the writer moves from one tense to another within the piece. I know I have been guilty, in the past, of telling my students "The verbs in your piece must all be in the same tense." Now, I realize that, as with most hard and fast 'rules,' exceptions can be used to good effect.

## Writing features to listen for

**FUNCTION** To inform.

**ORGANIZATION** Uses natural divisions of the topic. The writer divides the world into various cultures and tells what each of these cultures thinks of or how each explains the Milky Way. The writer arranges his information by geography and time; From Indo-European and ancient times to modern times.

Note the change from the past tense when writer tells of ancient cultures to the present tense when he tells of modern cultures.

**BEGINNING**
> **Hook:** Uses the word, *mysterious.* Appeals to universal interest in *early humans.*
>
> **Introduction:** First paragraph provides background information and tells reader what the rest of the piece will do: That is, it will tell you how different cultures answer the questions: What is the Milky Way? Where does it go? What is it made of?

**SUPPORTING DETAILS**
> **Definitions:** *Milky Way, a ribbon of light; Mecca, the holiest city of Islam; an emu (an ostrichlike bird).*

➠

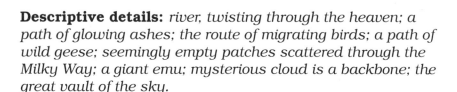 

**Descriptive details:** *river, twisting through the heaven; a path of glowing ashes; the route of migrating birds; a path of wild geese; seemingly empty patches scattered through the Milky Way; a giant emu; mysterious cloud is a backbone; the great vault of the sky.*

## LIVELY WRITING

**Strong verbs:** *gazed and wondered, considered, envisioned, marked, departing, has appearing, pictured, regarded, link, supporting, surrounded.*

**Repetition:** *. . . the mother of the sun and the mother of the moon.* Rather than: *. . . the mothers of the sun and moon.*

**Literary device: alliteration:** *mother's milk, stolen straw, picture it as a path, glowing ashes guiding, leading to the land.*

**TRANSITIONS** Because the writer presents so many different examples of cultures, he uses the transitional vocabulary of addition and contrast: *and, another, other, some, while other.*

**ENDING** An invitation to the reader to answer the questions for himself. *Next time you are surrounded by darkness on a clear night, look up at the Milky Way and imagine you don't know what it really is. What does it look like to you? What would you think of it if you lived long ago?* ☆

# Kids Who are Different

## by
## Digby Wolfe

Here's to the kids who are different,
The kids who don't always get A's,
The kids who have ears twice the size of their
    peers,
And noses that go on for days . . .
Here's to the kids who are different,
The kids they call crazy or dumb,
The kids who don't fit, with the guts and the
    grit,
Who dance to a different drum . . .
Here's to the kids who are different,
The kids with the mischievous streak,
For when they have grown, as history's shown,
It's their difference that makes them
    unique.  ☆

# Essay
## (Poem)

**"Kids Who are Different,"** by Digby Wolfe, was written for the 1992 CBS-TV special "Goldie," featuring Goldie Hawn, who read the poem. It has appeared in various publications including the Oct. 27, 1996 issue of *Parade Magazine.* Wolfe is an Emmy Award-winning writer and teaches dramatic writing at the University of New Mexico.

Yes, poems can be expository in nature. (Poems are commonly descriptive: "A Red, Red Rose" by Robert Burns or, narrative: "The Midnight Ride of Paul Revere" by Henry Wadsworth Longfellow, for example.) The writer of this piece offers his opinion and ideas about 'different kids,' in poetry form. He seeks our agreement, as most essay does.

## Writing features to listen for

**FUNCTION**  To state an opinion: to seek the reader's agreement.

**ORGANIZATION**  Metered and rhymed poetic form.

**SUPPORTING DETAILS**
**Descriptive details:** *don't get A's, ears twice the size of their peers, noses that go on for days, with guts and grit, dance to a different drum.*

**POETRY TECHNIQUES**
**Meter:** the eight-syllable pattern of lines 2, 4, 6, 8, and 10.
**Rhyme:** *ears-peers, A's -days, dumb-drum, grown-shown, streak-unique.*

**LIVELY WRITING**
**Hyperbole:** *ears twice the size of their peers; noses that go on for days*
**Idiom:** *dance to a different drum*
**Language:** Words chosen for their emotive value: *guts, grit*
**Repetition:** *Here's to the kids who are different.* (used three times)

➡

**ENDING** Circles back to the beginning using a variation on the same word: *different/difference.* Writer ends with the punch line; the conclusion the reader was waiting for to explain why the writer is saluting the kids who are different: *For when they have grown, as history's shown. It's their difference that makes them unique.* ✩

# Soaring with Books: Alicia's Link to a Better World

## by
## Bill Maxwell

Belle Glade, Florida

The journalist's instinct of taking a final look at everything in the area at the end of an interview caused me to notice seven-year-old Alicia Downing.

I was in this sugarcane growing town to write about an honor student at the local community college; the first member of her family — four generations of migrant farm workers — to attend college.

Having pocketed my notebook, stashed my tape recorder, slung my cameras over my shoulder and walked out the door of the apartment, I noticed the tiny figure at the end of the dingy breezeway.

There, at a picnic table, sat a girl. She was gripping a book, reading as if her very existence depended on it.

"That's my niece, Alicia," said Tonya Harvey, the student I had come to interview. "Alicia reads all the time. Sometimes she reads to me, and I read to her."

I automatically walked toward the child, snapped her picture and turned on my recorder.

"What's the name of the book you're reading?" I asked.

➥

"*Pocahontas,*" Alicia said. "She's an Indian girl. She lived a long time ago. She saved Capt. John Smith's life and became a princess and went to England. She's real pretty and has long, long hair. I like her. She's my favorite. I want to go to England, too."

For more than an hour, Alicia and I sat in the cool afternoon shade and talked. A second-grader at Pioneer Park Elementary School in Belle Glade, she enjoys reading more than anything else.

Why reading?

"It makes me happy," she said.

Even before she answered, I knew that the two of us were soul mates in many ways.

As a child, I, too, lived in Belle Glade. My family had been migrants and had cut sugar cane and picked vegetables here every season. I, too, had read most of the time.

Alicia lives with her grandmother. The drugs, violence, and other problems at their apartment complex have made life precarious for young children, and Alicia rarely ventures far from the front door without Tonya or her grandmother. Alicia finds refuge in books.

Reading connects her with the rest of the world — letting her share experiences common to people everywhere, taking her to distant lands that she may never actually visit, introducing her to ideas and information that will help her shape her views. Reading helps Alicia cope with the tragedies common to her environment.

➡

When talking about the joys of reading, Alicia uses words that flow like those of a character in a stream-of-consciousness drama: "I pick lots of books and read and read until I get tired; and when I read, I dream about going to the places I read about, and I dream about meeting some of the people and animals, too. In *Danny and the Dinosaur,* the little boy goes to lots of baseball games, and I like to go to baseball games. My cousin takes me sometimes."

She continues. "I read another book called *Chicken to Egg,* and I learned that a chick has to stay in the egg 21 days, and I read about snakes, and I'm scared of snakes, but I like to read about them. I'm going to read some more books about snakes. And when I grow up and get a job, I'm going to buy lots of books and let kids read them, and I want to write books for kids to read."

Reading is Alicia's anchor. It gives her peace of mind and helps ease the pain of being separated from her parents. Each afternoon after school, she submerges herself in the colorful pages of a book — a safe place where her imagination soars, where she can create ideal parents and friends, an orderly place where she is protected from harm, where she experiences certainty.

Instead of leaving Belle Glade with my usual sense of hopelessness, I left thrilled to have discovered another soul mate. And to my list of special people to whom I give books, I shall add the name of Alicia Downing. ✰

# Essay

## (Newspaper column)

**"Soaring with Books: Alicia's Link to a Better World,"** by Bill Maxwell, appeared in *the St. Petersburg Times,* St. Petersburg, Florida on November 2, 1996. Maxwell is a columnist for *The Times.* He writes passionately about books, literacy, and the intellectual life.

Personal experience influenced my choice of this essay. Like Alicia Downing and Bill Maxwell, I, too, found refuge in books as a child. This piece demonstrates how an essay, writing about ideas, can be devoted almost entirely to a story; how a narrative can speak so strongly in support of a main idea, here, "soaring with books." The story validates the writer's ideas — proves his point.

This piece reveals a writer who is passionate about his subject. The story provides the setting in which the writer can express that passion. Instead of talking in the abstract about the value of reading, the writer takes us to a real place, to meet a real child, to show us the value of reading.

When you read this piece to your students have them find, amidst the narrative, the expository elements that drive the piece.

## Writing features to listen for

**FUNCTION** To present and illustrate an idea. The writer states that idea in the title: "Soaring with Books: Alicia's Link to a Better World." This also serves as the hook.

**ORGANIZATION** Primarily narrative with the writer's expository ideas and conclusions placed throughout the piece.
> **The expository writing:** The writer tells us that reading connects Alicia with the rest of the world; Reading helps Alicia cope with the tragedies common to her environment; Reading is Alicia's anchor; Writer recognized child as a soul mate, a reader like him.

➥

Alicia talks about her reading in an expository style as well. She expresses her feelings about books: *I read, I dream, I like to go, When I grow up.*

**BEGINNING**

**Introduction:** Setting and background information. The writer is in Belle Glade, Florida to do an interview and discovers a soul mate.

**Lively Writing:**

**Strong verbs:** *pocketed, stashed, slung, noticed, gripping, depended, snapped, ventures, connects, cope, ease, submerges, soars, create, thrilled.*

**Descriptive details:** *sugar-cane growing town, tiny figure, gripping a book, dingy breezeway, picnic table, cool of the afternoon shade.*

**Literary devices:**

**Simile:** . . . *she enjoys reading more than anything else.*

**Analogy:** *As a child, I, too, lived in Belle Glade. I, too, had read most of the time.*

**Opposites:** Soaring: *Why reading? "It makes me happy," she said; safe place where her imagination soars.* Anchored: *Reading connects her with the rest of the world. Reading is Alicia's anchor...*

**Language:** Words chosen for their emotive value: *joys of reading, cause the pain, soul mates, made life precarious, imagination soars, sense of hopelessness.*

**ENDING** Writer sums up how he feels about the subject: *Instead of leaving Belle Glade with my usual sense of hopelessness, I left thrilled to have discovered another soul mate. And to my list of special people to whom I give books, I shall add the name of Alicia Downing.*

He brings back the name of the town, Belle Glade, to echo his beginning. ☆

# An Idea for a Safer Bee Ridge

## by
## Robert H. Brown

Concerning the numerous vehicle accidents on Bee Ridge Road: Bee Ridge Road reminds me of a similar "death road" — Route 22 in New Jersey. That, too, is a heavily traveled, multi-lane, commercialized thoroughfare.

But Route 22 is relatively safe now. Concrete barriers down the center of it stopped the practice of drivers braving three lanes of traffic to make a left turn from driveways and businesses lining the highway.

This is what drivers continually attempt on Bee Ridge Road. We know the result.

It is time to stop the carnage on Bee Ridge Road. It is time to create sensible driving patterns on this death road. A concrete barrier down the center, limiting crossover access, will do much to make it safer for all of us.  ☆

# Opinion/Persuasive Essay

## (Letter-to-the-Editor)

**"An Idea for A Safer Bee Ridge,"** by Robert H. Brown appeared as a letter-to-the-editor in the *Sarasota Herald Tribune* on November 25, 1996.

I like the way the author uses an analogy to support his position. The piece is short, succinct, and to the point, with no extraneous information.

### Writing features to listen for

**FUNCTION** To air an opinion. To convince the public and persuade officials to take action.

**ORGANIZATION** Problem and solution through use of analogy: Bee Ridge is just like Route 22 in New Jersey. Let's make Bee Ridge safe the same way Route 22 was made safe.

**BEGINNING**
> **Hook:** A sentence fragment: *Concerning the numerous vehicle accidents on Bee Ridge Road:*
>
> In memo style, Mr. Brown states the problem: numerous accidents.

**ARGUMENT** Appeals to common values: *safe for all of us.*

**SUPPORTING DETAILS**
> **Comparison:** *Bee Ridge Road reminds me of a similar "death road" — Route 22 in New Jersey. That, too, is a heavily traveled, multi-lane, commercialized thoroughfare.*
>
> **Descriptive details:** *heavily traveled, multi-lane, commercialized; concrete barriers down the center.*

**FOCUS**
> Succinct writing with simple description of the problem and a solution. No extra material. Letters-to-the-editor should be brief and to the point.

➡

**LIVELY WRITING**

**People-oriented:** Uses *we, you, us.*

**Active voice and strong verbs:** Concrete barriers *stopped* the practice; drivers *braving;* drivers *attempt; create* sensible driving patterns.

**Repetition for emphasis:** *It is time to . . . , It is time to . . .*

**Short paragraphs and sentence length variation:** Only one paragraph is over two sentences long.

**LANGUAGE** Words chosen for their emotive value: *death road, drivers braving three lanes, carnage.*

**ENDING** The writer offers a solution: *A concrete barrier down the center, limiting crossover access, will do much to make it safer for all of us.* ☆

# Next Stop Sub Station!

## by
## Rita Mazer

When you've got the munchies, there's no better way to ease your hunger pangs than a trip to Sub Station.

There's usually a Sub Station right around the corner. And, best of all, you don't have to dress up. Just throw on a pair of shorts and go!

Ummm... just think of those huge sandwiches filled with layers of turkey and ham, bacon and cheese, bologna and beef... Smothered with your choice of slivered onions, lettuce, peppers, olives, tomatoes, vinegar, and oil. And don't forget the jalapenos to give it that extra zing! Makes your mouth water just thinking about it.

You can afford it, too. A 6" Cold Cut Trio with ham, salami, and bologna, plus all the "fixins" is just $1.89. If you're smart, you'll look for the Sub Station coupons in your local newspaper that advertise, "Buy One...Get One Free with Purchase of a Drink." Speaking of drinks, you get free refills at Sub Station.

Last week, I stopped in after school and ordered a 6" Classic Italian BMT loaded with ham, Genoa salami, pepperoni, pickles, lettuce and tomato for just $2.69. My girlfriend, who always goes for the veggies and sprouts, got the Vegetarian Special, chock full of all those things that are so good for you. Just $2.39! We like the fact that they prepare the sandwiches right in front of you. And they bake their rolls every four hours so the bread is always nice and fresh!

➡

We both agreed Sub Station is the place to go with a date after the movies or a football game. See you there! ☆

*Read-Aloud Samples*

# Persuasive Writing

## (Advertisement)

**"Next Stop Sub Station,"** by Rita Mazer, is modeled after the author's restaurant reviews which appear weekly in the *Sarasota Herald Tribune.* Her column, "Food For Thought," features paid-for reviews, called advertorials (advertisements in an editorial format).

I selected this piece to show how a writer chooses the language and tone that suits her audience. This review is designed to persuade teenagers to eat at The Sub Station. I recommend that you hold off reading this piece to your students until after lunch.

### Writing features to listen for

**FUNCTION**   To describe and persuade.

### BEGINNINGS

**Hook:** Title: Play on words: *Next Stop Sub Station!* Mimics a conductor calling out a train station.

**Introduction:** Talks directly to all hungry teenagers. *When you've got the munchies, there's no better way to ease your hunger pangs than a trip to Sub Station.*

### ARGUMENTS

**Appeal to vanity:** *If you're smart, you'll look for the Sub Station coupons . . .*

**Appeal to social status:** *Sub Station is the place to go with a date after the movies or a football game.*

**Benefits to reader:**
    **Easy:** *There's usually a Sub Station right around the corner in your own neighborhood. And, best of all, you don't have to dress up. Just throw on a pair of shorts and go!*

    **Economical:** *You can afford it, too.*

    **Healthful:** *My girlfriend, who always goes for the veggies and sprouts, got the Vegetarian Special, chock full of all those things that are so good for you.*

➥

## SUPPORTING DETAILS

**Descriptive details:** . . . *layers of turkey and ham, bacon and cheese, bologna and beef; Smothered with your choice of slivered onions, lettuce, peppers, olives, tomatoes, vinegar, and oil. And don't forget the jalapenos to give it that extra zing!; The bread is always nice and fresh!*

**Proof:** *You can afford it, too. A 6" Cold Cut Trio with ham, salami, and bologna, plus all the "fixins," is just $1.89.*

**Specific details:** Prices in dollar and cents, free drink refills, ingredients, names of sandwiches

**Numbers:** *A 6" Cold Cut Trio is just $1.89; Just $2.39!*

**Narrative vignette:** *Last week, I stopped in after school and ordered a 6" Classic Italian BMT loaded with ham, Genoa salami, pepperoni, pickles, lettuce and tomato for just $2.69. My girlfriend, who always goes for the veggies and sprouts, got the Vegetarian Special . . .*

## LIVELY WRITING

**Talks directly to reader:** using *you, I, us, we.*

**People-oriented:** *My girlfriend and I, See you there.*

**Language and tone suited for audience:** Casual: *fixins, date, munchies*

Words chosen for their emotive value: *smothered with your choice of; extra zing; mouth water.*

**Syllabic rhythm:** Listen to the syllabic pattern in the pairs of ingredients: 2 (or 3) syllables, then the word *and*, followed with one syllable, creating a fid-dle, dee, dee rhythm: *tur-key and ham, ba-con and cheese, bo-log-na and beef.* (Imagine if Dr. Seuss had called his book, *Ham and Green Eggs!*)

## PERSUASIVE TECHNIQUES

**Reiteration:** Name of the restaurant, *Sub Station* (repeated five times) and ingredients of the subs.

**Current:** *Last week I stopped in . . .*

**ENDING** Circles back to the hook; in content and punctuation. Title: *Next Stop Sub Station!*, Ending: *See you there!* Also relates to the beginning statement: *There's no better way to ease your hunger pangs than a trip to Sub Station.* Ending: *Sub Station is the place to go.* ☆

# The Pier,
# St. Petersburg, Florida

The excitement grows as you approach — the speedboats race by, while a gentle breeze billows the colorful sails of a catamaran. Private planes buzz into the neighboring executive airport. An old-fashioned trolley in tropical hues pulls up to The Pier — five stories of fun, food, shopping and more — right on the waterfront, in downtown St. Petersburg, Florida.

Hands-on educational  exhibits from the Great Explorations Museum, live musical entertainment, boat shows — there's always something going on at The Pier. And with so much to do and see: galleries, specialty shops, boutiques and more, you're sure to work up an appetite.

So go ahead, grab some popcorn, a burger or ice cream cone. The mouthwatering smells from the Food Court are hard to resist! Or, have a seat in an elegant eatery like the famed Columbia, and indulge in the area's most acclaimed Spanish cuisine. You can choose to eat inside-cozy or outside-casual by the bay at Nick's on the Water, an Italian/Seafood restaurant.

Wherever you go, sparkling water views surround and inspire you. Take it all in from the top-floor observation deck. The brilliant Florida sunset, the sailboats and ships heading out to sea... the unique and panoramic look at the City of St. Petersburg.

So come spend the day at The Pier. Come play the waterfront way! ☆

# Persuasive Writing

## (Advertisement)

**"The Pier, St. Petersburg, Florida,"** is a travel brochure from W.H.G. Management, Inc. which graciously permitted its reprinting.

I selected this piece to demonstrate the language of advertising. This ad uses detailed description of the product in language that appeals to our senses and emotions and makes us want to go there. Spend time with this piece and savor the words the author selected.

The author of this ad uses an incomplete sentence for effect (in the next-to-last paragraph), just as the writer of the Camp Fish advertisement did.

### Writing features to listen for

**FUNCTION**  To describe and persuade.

**DESCRIPTION**
 **Descriptive attributes:** sights, sounds, smells, feelings.
 **Strong verbs:** *race, billows, buzz, work up an appetite, grab, resist, indulge, choose, surround, inspire, spend.*
 **Adjectives with emotive value:** *gentle, private, old-fashioned, hands-on, mouthwatering, elegant, inside-cozy, casual, sparkling, brilliant, unique and panoramic, waterfront.*

**LIVELY WRITING**
 **Specificity and use of proper nouns:** *colorful sails of a catamaran, from the Great Explorations Museum, from the Food Court, the famed Columbia, Nick's on the Water*
 **Literary devices:**
  **Alliteration:** *breeze billows, private planes, trolleys in tropical hues, five stories of fun and food, educational exhibits, so go, elegant eatery, sunset, sailboats and ships heading out to sea, waterfront way.*
  **Onomatopoeia:** *buzz*

➥

## PERSUASIVE ARGUMENTS

**Appeal to reader's appetite:** *popcorn, a burger or ice cream cone; The mouthwatering smells from the Food Court are hard to resist!; . . . indulge in the area's most acclaimed Spanish cuisine.*

**Appeal to common values:**

- Education: *Hands-on educational exhibits from the Great Explorations Museum.*
- Common interests: shopping, being where the action is, eating.

## SUPPORTING DETAILS

**Concrete examples:** So much to do and see: *galleries, specialty shops, boutiques and more . . .* Take it all in*: The brilliant Florida sunset, the sailboats and ships heading out to sea . . . St. Petersburg.*

**ENDING** An alliterative summary and invitation, using the summary transition word, *so.*

So come spend the <u>day</u> at The Pier. Come <u>play</u> the waterfront <u>way</u>! ☆

# How the Stock Market Works

## by
## Michael Charles

You opened a lemonade stand this summer. It was hard work, but it was fun and you made some money. Next summer, you'd like to set up several stands around the neighborhoods near your home. The only trouble is, you don't have enough money to build the other stands. Looks like you're stuck.

Then you think: Hey, what if I ask my parents and some of their friends to advance me the money to build the chain of stands. In return, I'll pay them a share of my profits. And that's what you do.

The next summer, twenty people each give you $10. In return, you give each of them a piece of paper that says he or she owns a part of your lemonade business. With the $200, you build a bunch of stands. Several of your friends agree to run the new stands for you for 20% of the dollars of lemonade they sell. You're in business.

At the end of that summer, you have a nice profit after paying for the lemons and sugar and your friends' help. You put aside enough money to build more stands, improve the signs on all your existing stands, and pay for next year's lemonade ingredients. After paying yourself to make your work and worry worthwhile, you have enough left to pay 50 cents to each of the twenty people who put $10 into the business. They are happy — that's more than they would have earned if they had saved that $10 in the bank.

➡

One of these people, however, is going to move away. Rather than keep her share in your business, she decides to sell it. Someone agrees to buy it for $12. That's more than the original owner paid for it because now, everyone can see that your business is doing well, getting bigger, and paying a nice amount at the end of the summer. So, the person who is moving away not only earned 50 cents on her $10, but made an extra $2 by selling her share of the business. Not bad for one year!

What you did with your lemonade stand is exactly what companies known as **corporations** do. These companies sell hamburgers, furniture, cars, services — all the things people want and need. If people don't want or need the company's product, or if the products are of poor quality, people won't buy them. And the company will go out of business. If the company's products are useful and well-made, people will buy a lot of them, and the company will grow.

It takes money to grow, however. Just as with your lemonade stands, new stores or factories cost a lot of money to build. One way for corporations to get this growth money is to sell **shares** in their business to **investors**, just as you did. The investors get a piece of paper, called **stock**, that tells them how much of the company they own — just like the piece of paper you gave to your investors.

The corporation pays its investors a portion of its profit each year, as a **dividend**. If the company's profits grow, owning a share in it becomes more valuable, and investors can sell their share for more than they paid for it, as did the lemonade-stand investor who moved away. Of course, if the company does

➡

badly, its stock will become less valuable, and if the company goes out of business, its stock will have no value. So you would want to buy stock only in strong companies that are likely to stay in business and grow.

Because there are many thousands of corporations and many millions of investors, it could be difficult for shareholders to find someone to sell their shares to, or for new investors to buy shares. To ease this process, there is a **stock market**. Every day, some investors tell the market how many shares they'd like to sell and the price they are asking. Other investors tell the market how many shares of a company they want to buy and how much they're willing to pay. The market matches up the sellers and the buyers. Everyday in the newspaper, you can see how many shares of each company were **traded** on the previous day and at what price. ☆

# Exposition

## (Explanation)

**"How the Stock Market Works,"** was written expressly for this book by Michael Charles who is an editor, a retired corporate vice-president, and an investor.

I selected this piece for the way the writer explains something pretty complicated by showing readers how it is similar to something they might already know, i.e., by using an analogy. Though the stock market is a complex subject, the writer makes it easy for students to understand by using friendly language and defining new terms in relation to what readers know or might have experienced.

## Writing features to listen for

**FUNCTION**  To explain.

**ORGANIZATION**  Problem-and-solution format. The writer constructs an analogy to define and explain the stock market by describing the development of the lemonade business and corporations.

**BEGINNING**
   **Hook:** Writer talks directly to the reader.

   **Introduction:** A problem is described: a hypothetical but likely personal situation (raising money to expand a small business) that a reader may have experienced or can relate to.

**SUPPORTING DETAILS**
   **Defines new terms:** corporation, investor, share, stock, dividend, stock market — through comparison to the lemonade business. *(What you did; . . . just like the piece of paper; Just as with your lemonade; . . . as did the lemonade investor; . . . just as you did.)*

   **Extended narrative example:** The lemonade-stand scenario.

   **Use of numbers:** dollars, percents

➡

**Concrete examples:** *These companies sell hamburgers, furniture, cars; lemonade ingredients, lemons and sugar,*

## LIVELY WRITING

**Writer talks to you:** *Looks like you're stuck!; Not bad for one year!; Then you think, Hey,; And, that's what you do; You're in business.*

**Active voice:** People, not things, are the subjects of sentences: *Every day you can see how many shares.* Not: Everyday the newspaper lists the shares . . .

**Alliteration:** *set up several stands, build a bunch, many millions, price the investor paid, a portion of its profits, work and worry worthwhile.*

**Contractions:** Gives writing a conversational, informal tone: *you'd, don't, you're, I'll, that's.*

## TRANSITIONS

**Time transition vocabulary:** *Then, Next summer, At the end of the summer.*

**Transition technique:** Using words in the last sentence of one paragraph to introduce the next paragraph material. Examples: From paragraph 2 to 3: *. . . build a bunch of **stands**. The next summer, several of your friends agree to run the new **stands**;* From paragraph 5 to 6: *. . . the company will **grow**. But it takes money **to grow**;* From paragraph 6 to 7: *. . . you gave to your **investors**. The corporation pays its **investors**...*

**ENDING** Suprisingly, the first mention of the stock market, which is what the title says the piece is about, does not come until the final paragraph. The writer had to introduce the reader to many concepts and terms before he could effectively explain the stock market. Imagine the final paragraph as a first paragraph — the reader would most likely not understand a thing it says.

Notice that the writer does not have a formal concluding sentence such as, *That is how the stock market works.* He doesn't need one. The piece was titled "How the Stock Market Works," and in the final paragraph he delivers that promise, based on the information he provided earlier in the article. ☆

# Art and Music

### by
### Mischa Abshire

Sarasota County is in danger of losing an important segment of the arts community: its future audience and its future performers. The arts programs in many of our county schools have been taken away.

This is a tragedy. For many students, school is the only place to learn and enjoy art and music, the only way to be exposed to art and music. Not only is it a wonderful and memorable experience, it is also a lot of fun.

Art and music are often the favorite subjects of many students. Some students do not excel in math and English but have artistic abilities that must be acknowledged and praised. If the art and music programs are taken out of the elementary schools, many children will be deprived of the chance to excel in the arts.

Sarasota is an arts-oriented community, which makes the removal of the arts programs particularly ironic. Sarasota is known as the cultural center of Florida. Artists, musicians, dancers, and writers make it their home — come here for that very reason. Our community has so much to offer in the areas of art, music, theater and ballet; it is a shame to waste this knowledge.

If we want our art community to flourish, we need to expand our art and music programs, not eliminate them. ☆

# Persuasive Essay
## (Letter-to-the-editor: Student piece)

**"Art and Music,"** by Mischa Abshire, a tenth grader. This student writer uses a good number of emotive words to enhance her arguments and convey her depth of feeling about the topic.

<u>**Writing features to listen for**</u>

**FUNCTION**  To persuade.

**ORGANIZATION**  Standard persuasive form: opinion, arguments supported by specific details, a conclusion including a proposal.

**BEGINNING**
> **Hook:** a warning. *Sarasota County is in danger . . .*
>
> **Introduction:** Background information: *. . . arts programs are being eliminated.*
>
> **Opinion:** *This is a tragedy.*

**ARGUMENTS**
> **Appeals to common values:**
> - Sense of fairness: *For many students, school is the only place to learn and enjoy art and music, the only way to be exposed to art and music.*
> - Rewarding merit: *artistic abilities must be acknowledged and praised; kids must have the chance to excel . . .*
> - Waste not, want not: *if we want our community to flourish . . . a shame to waste . . .*
>
> **Appeals to emotion:** *Not only is it* (taking art and music) *a wonderful and memorable experience, it is also a lot of fun.*

**SUPPORTING DETAILS**
> **Facts:** *For many students, school is the only place to learn and enjoy art and music, the only way to be exposed to art and music; Artists, musicians, dancers, and writers make it* (Sarasota) *their home.*

➡

## LIVELY WRITING

**Language:** Words chosen for their connotative and emotive values: Negative connotation: *deprived, shame, waste.* Emotive: *danger, memorable, flourish, ironic.*

**Alliteration:** *artistic abilities, cultural center.*

**ENDING**  Final argument, the clincher, appeals to common values: *If we want our community to flourish . . .* And, the writer proposes a solution, using opposites for impact: *expand, . . . not eliminate.*  ✫

# Don't Run with Those Scissors!

### by
### David Grimes

Today is Mother's Day, which seems like a good time for us to review and evaluate some of the well-intentioned advice that our mothers passed along to us when we were kids.

For example:

*Don't run with those scissors in your hand.* Judging by how often this warning was repeated, we must have spent an unusual amount of our childhood galloping around the house, waving pinking shears over our heads. I don't remember my mother warning me to not run around with anything else, such as a meat cleaver, live hand grenade, or poisonous snakes.

Which begs the question: What were all those scissors doing lying around where we could get our hands on them? Anyway, you don't often see grownups running around with scissors in their hand, so I guess our mothers did a good job.

*Cigarette smoking will stunt your growth.* Given the fact that our mothers had no qualms about scaring us to death in order to get their points across, I find it odd that they said, "Cigarette smoking will stunt your growth" instead of, "Cigarette smoking will kill you." Perhaps, in those days, we were more afraid of being short than dead.

*Eat everything on your plate because people are starving in China.* OK, let me see if I've got

➡

this right: For every minute that I spend pushing my lima beans around my plate, 100,000 in China drop dead from starvation. Does this mean that if I eat my beans, the people of China are suddenly transformed into chubby, little butterballs? If one little lima bean can make such a difference, then, by all means, Mom, let's race down to the post office this very minute and airmail that sucker straight to Guandong, or the province of your choice.

*Always wear clean underwear in case you're in an accident and have to go to the hospital.* Encouraging children to wear clean underwear is all well and good, but I'm not sure the hospital argument is the way to go about it. For one thing, the first thing they do to you at the hospital is make you take off all your clothes, dirty underwear and all, and put on one of those awful hospital gowns made by some of those lima bean-deprived Chinese who keeled over from hunger before they could finish the rear half of the gown. Furthermore, I suspect that the hospital administration would not care if you showed up in dirty underwear so long as you had proof of medical insurance. ☆

# Humorous Essay

## (Humor newspaper column)

**"Don't Run with Those Scissors!"** by David Grimes, appeared in the *Sarasota Herald Tribune* on Mother's Day, 1995. Grimes writes a regular humorous column for that paper.

I selected this piece because it demonstrates how a writer can make us laugh by observing the folly of some common human behaviors, looking at the familiar with new and humorous eyes. The writer does this by asking outrageous questions, pointing out the ridiculous, and using hyperbole and funny language.

## Writing features to listen for

**FUNCTION**  To amuse.

**ORGANIZATION**  A list.

**BEGINNING**
**Hook:** Refers to a holiday: *Today is Mother's Day.* The remainder of the first sentence tweaks our curiosity to see if this will apply to us and our moms: *. . . which seems like a good time for us to review and evaluate some of the well-intentioned advice that our mothers passed along to us when we were kids. For example:*
**Introduction:** The writer tells us what he is going to do and why.

**TRANSITIONS**  The writer need no transitions between paragraph because he promised a list.

**LIVELY, HUMOROUS WRITING**
**People-oriented:** Use of *I* and *you, people in China.*
**Talks directly to the reader and asks questions:** *What were all those scissors doing lying around where we could get our hands on them?; OK, let me see if I've got this right; Does this mean that if I eat my beans, the people of China are suddenly transformed into chubby, little butterballs?*

➡

**Specificity, including use of numbers:** *pinking shears; straight to Guandong; 100,000 in China*

**Strong verbs:** *galloping around, waving pinking shears, I spend, pushing my limas, transformed, race, keel over, I suspect.*

**Funny words or expressions that make us smile:** *galloping around, scaring us to death, chubby little butterballs, mail that sucker straight to Guandong, or the province of your choice.*

**Literary devices:**

> **Hyperbole and the outrageous:** *. . . meat cleavers, hand grenades, poisonous snakes; Perhaps, in those days, we were more afraid of being short that dead; lima bean-deprived Chinese who keeled over from hunger before they could finish the rear half of the gown; Furthermore, I suspect that the hospital administration would not care if you showed up in dirty underwear so long as you had proof of medical insurance.*

> **Alliteration:** *drop dead; by all means, Mom; mail that sucker straight; could finish the rear half.*

**ENDING** The writer ties together the last two pieces of mothers' advice in a funny way: the starving, lima bean-deprived Chinese workers who can't sew up the back of the dreaded hospital gown. Then he finishes with a punchline, a humorous non sequitur that plays on the universal fear of a stupendous hospital bill. He leaves us laughing and fully satisfied without a formal summary. ✩

# Big Words are for the Birds

## by
## Joseph A. Ecclesine

When you come right down to it, there is no law that says you have to use big words when you write or talk.

There are lots of small words, and good ones, that can be made to say all the things you want to say, quite as well as the big ones. It may take a bit more time to find them at first, but it can be well worth it (since we all know what they mean). Some small words, more than you think, are rich with just the right feel, the right taste, as if made to help you say a thing the way it should be said.

Small words can be crisp, brief, terse — they go right to the point, like a knife. They have a charm all their own. They dance, twist, turn, and sing. Like sparks in the night they light the way for the eyes of those who read. They are the grace notes of prose. You know what they say the same way you know a day is bright and clear — at first sight. You find, as you read, that you like the way they say it. Small words are fun. They can catch large thoughts and hold them for all to see, like rare stones in rings of gold, or joy in the eyes of a child. Some make you "feel," as well as see: the cold deep dark of night, the hot salt sting of tears.

Small words move with ease where big words stand still (or worse, bog down and get in the way of what you want to say). In all truth, there is not much that small words will not say and say quite well. ☆

# Persuasive Essay

**"Big Words are for The Birds,"** by Joseph A. Ecclesine, appeared in "Printer's Ink," February 17, 1961. The sample is adapted from this essay.

Share this persuasive piece with your middle-school and high-school student writers. As I have indicated previously, elementary students are not ready for this aspect of refining their writing: weighing every word. They already write with small words. They would take this advice literally and stop expanding their writing vocabularies. They are developing fluency and need to use every word at their disposal, large and small.

But, more advanced writers can enjoy this persuasive piece for its construction, details, the evident enjoyment of the author, and the clever technique he used to support his contention: Big Words Are for the Birds. See if your students catch the trick Ecclesine used.

## Writing features to listen for

**FUNCTION**  To persuade and amuse.

**ORGANIZATION**  Standard persuasive structure: Opinion, two arguments supported with details, and clincher and restatement of opinion as an ending.

### BEGINNING
**The hook:** The hook is the title. The writer uses an idiom, *"for the birds."*

**The statement of opinion:** *. . . there is no law that says you have to use big words when you write or talk.*

### ARGUMENTS
**Appeal to practicality:** *There are lots of small words, and good ones, that can be made to say all the things you want to say, quite as well as the big ones. It may take a bit more time to find them at first, but it can be well worth it (since we all know what they mean).*

➡

**Appeal to aesthetics, emotions:** *Some small words, more than you think, are rich with just the right feel, the right taste, as if made to help you say a thing the way it should be said.*

## SUPPORTING DETAILS

**Descriptive details:** *Small words can be crisp, brief, terse; They dance, twist, turn, and sing; the cold deep dark of night; the hot salt sting of tears.*

## LIVELY WRITING

**Talks to the reader:** *When you come right down to it, there is no law that says you have to use big words when you write or talk. And, You know what they say the same way you know a day is bright and clear — at first sight. You find, as you read, that you like the way they say it.*

**Strong verbs:** *Small words . . . dance, twist, turn, and sing; They light the way; They catch large thoughts...*

**Language:** All the words are one syllable to illustrate and emphasize the author's point: small words can do it all. How can you disagree after hearing this piece?

**Literary devices:**

**Simile:** *go right to the point like a knife; like sparks in the night they light the way; like rare stones in rings of gold; like joy in the eyes of a child.*

**Metaphor:** *They are the grace notes of prose.*

**ENDING** A one-sentence clinching argument, and one sentence of thesis reiteration. ☆

# Sources for Further Read-Aloud Samples

## Elementary

### Books

Aliotti, Shelley. *My Pen Pal Scrapbook.* Tiburon, CA: World View Publishers, 1995.

Bash, Barbara. *Desert Giant: The World Of The Saquaro Cactus.* Boston, MA: Little Brown and Co./ San Francisco, CA: Sierra Club Books, 1989.

Broekel, Ray. *I Can Be An* Author. Chicago, IL: Childrens Press, 1986.

Chesanow, Neil. *Where Do I Live?* New York, NY: Barron's, 1995.

Colman, Warren. *The Bill Of Rights.* Chicago, IL: Children's Press, 1987.

Detz, Joan. *You Mean I Have To Stand Up And Say Something?* New York, NY: Atheneum, 1986.

Dorros, Arthur. *Ant Cities.* New York, NY: Thomas W. Crowell, 1987.

Erlbach, Arlene. *The Best Friends Book.* Minneapolis, MN: Free Spirit Publishing, 1995.

Gibbons, Gail. *The Milk Makers.* New York, NY: Macmillan Publishing Co., 1995.

Kalb, Jonah and Viscott, David. *What Every Kid Should Know.* Boston, MA: Houghton Mifflin, 1976 .

Kaufman, Elizabeth E. *Monkeys and Apes.* Los Angeles, CA: Price/ Stern/Sloan, 1986.

Kennet, Frances and Measham, Terry. *Looking at Paintings.* New York, NY: Marshall Cavendish, 1989.

Koehler, Lora. *Internet.* Chicago, IL: Children's Press, 1995.

Langley, Andrew. *Energy.* New York, NY: Bookwright Press, 1986.

Leokum, Arkady. *Tell Me Why #5.* New York, NY: Grosset and Dunlap, 1988.

Lepthien, Emilie U. *Manatees.* Chicago, IL: Children's Press, 1991.

Maestro, Betsy. *The Story of Money.* New York, NY: A Mulberry Paperback Book, 1993.

Parker, Nancy Winslow and Wright, Joan Richards. *Bugs.* New York, NY: Green Willow Books, 1987.

Patent, Dorothy Hinshaw. *All About Whales.* New York, NY: Holiday House, 1987.

Peterson, Jenne Whitehouse. *I Have A Sister, My Sister Is Deaf.* New York, NY: Harper and Row Publishers, 1977.

Srivastava, Jane Jonas. *Statistics.* New York, NY: Thomas Y. Cromwell, 1973.

Pickering, Robert B. *I Can Be An Archeologist.* Chicago, IL: Children's Press, 1987.

Sipiera, Paul P. *I Can Be An Oceanographer.* Chicago, IL: Children's Press, 1987.

## Reading Rainbow books

Scieszka, Jon and Smith, Lane. *Math Curse.* New York, NY: Viking, 1995.

Stock, Gregory, *The Kid's Book of Questions.* New York, NY: Workman Publishing Co., Inc., 1988.

Gibbons, Gail. *Knights in Shining Armor.* New York, NY: Little Brown and Co., 1995.

## Magazines

*American Girl*
*Boys' Life*
*Children's Digest*
*Cricket Magazine*
*Highlights*
*Hopscotch For Girls*
*Ice Skating Institute of America*
*Jack and Jill*
*National Geographic World*
*Odyssey*
*Owl*
*Ranger Rick*
*Super Science 4-5-6*
*US Kids*
*Youth 95*
*Zillions: Consumer Reports For Kids*

# Middle/High School

## Books

Essay sources can be found in the non-fiction section of your library, Dewey Decimal numbers 814, 817, and 824.

Baker, Russell. *The Rescue of Miss Yaskell and Other Pipe Dreams.* New York, NY: Congdon and Weed, Inc., 1983.

Baker, Russell. *There's a Country In My Cellar.* New York, NY: William Morrow and Co., 1990.

Brodsky, Joseph. *On Grief and Reason: Essays.* New York, NY: Farrar Straus Giroux, 1995.

Detz, Joan. *You Mean I Have To Stand Up And Say Something?* New York, NY: Atheneum, 1986.

Feldman, David. *Imponderables.* New York, NY: William Morrow and Co., Inc., 1986.

Morrow, Anne. *Gift From the Sea.* New York, NY: Pantheon Book, 1995. "The Beach."

White, E.B. *The Essays of E. B. White.* New York, NY: Harper & Row Publishers, 1971, Page 205: "The Sea and The Wind That Blows."

## Magazines

*Cobblestone: History magazine for young people*

*Faces: Magazine About People (Cobblestone and Museum Of Natural History, NY)*

*New Horizons: Future Farmers of America*

*Horse and Rider*

*Nintendo Power*

*Dog Fancy*

*BMX Plus*

*American Girl*

*Racing For Kids*

*Sports Illustrated for Kids*

# Appendix I

## Some Tips from the Pros for Young Expository Writers

Here are some writing tips professionals commonly offer novices. I advise young writers to read their rough drafts through, checking for one tip at a time. I tell them, for example, "If you are checking to see that your sentences are different lengths, count the words per sentence. If the pattern is something like: 6, 6, 5, 5, 6, 6, 5, 6, 6 . . . your reader might fall asleep from boredom. Consider combining a few sentences or extending others with more details."

I suggest an additional read-through, to check for specific nouns. "Did you use *store*, or *Sports Authority?* Did you use *snack* or *peanuts?*" And so forth.

Multiple readings are also a good way to proofread a final draft for spelling, punctuation, and capitalization — one convention at a time.

## Tips

Write like you talk.
Picture your reader.
Use specific nouns and strong verbs.
Prefer the active rather than the passive voice.
Choose the positive rather than the negative. (*Remember . . .* instead of, *Do not forget . . .*)
Provide facts.
Help your reader see what you see, using descriptive details and comparisons.
Vary your sentence length.
Master the simple declarative sentence.
Try not to over use any one kind of punctuation. (Exclamations do not make your writing more exciting.)
Write your titles, beginnings and endings last.
Keep your paragraphs short.
Remember, the reader is rarely at fault when the text is misunderstood.

# Appendix II

**Lesson: Organizing an informational piece by physically clumping related information.**

This classroom demonstration works well with writers as young as second-grade for their introduction to informational expository and with older students (fifth or sixth grade) as a precursor to the abstract task of outlining. Young writers need concrete means to organize their information. They need to do this before they can independently create abstract graphic planners such as webs, clusters, or maps.

During immersion in a topic, provide each student with ten or more 14" x 4" strips of paper or a large piece of drawing paper lined every 4 inches. Ask them to record facts they learn or ideas they have about the topic on these strips, one sentence per strip.

Independent writers should add sentence strips of information each day. Emergent writers can copy sentences from environmental text, or dictate them to you or another child. Give your students time to read their sentence strips to each other often. The reading will reinforce the concept of complete sentences and spread information about the topic through the class.

At the close of the immersion period, gather the class for a demonstration of sorting and classifying. Model with buttons, thinking aloud as you sort your collection: e.g., *I'm putting all the ones with two holes in one pile, and all the ones with four holes in another.* Have students do the same with various sets of objects, such as playing cards, sea shells, toys. Call on children to tell their classmates *how* they are sorting their objects — *"I put all the red cards in one pile and all the black ones in the other." Or, "I put all the picture cards in one pile and all the rest in the other."* Repeat the sorting procedure to form three divisions. Make it clear to students that they may use many different sorting schemes.

Next, show your students how to sort their strips of topic information in the same fashion. Model with your own prepared strips. Spread your strips on the floor or large table and gather the class around you. Sort the pieces of information, thinking aloud, and physically moving the information around. *"This is about what whales look like, but this one is about eating krill. I'll put them in two piles. This one is about how*

*big they are. I think I'll put that in the pile about how they look."*
Continue until all your strips are in three piles.

If you have some that do not fit in the three or four piles you formed, set them aside. Tell your students they might have one or two left over when they sort their information. Extra strips that do not naturally fall into one of the piles may be discarded, traded, or used to start a new pile.

Ask the children to sort their own information strips. Rove around and help children read and sort their strips. With second-graders, you might choose to work with half the class at a time.

After sorting, have children paste their piles of information in clumps on a sheet of newsprint. Model with your own. *"I am going to paste the ones about what whales look like first."* Help kids do the same. The youngest writers may not arrange the piles in logical order but that's OK. Let them choose their own layout.

Caption: A young writer pastes clumps of related information.

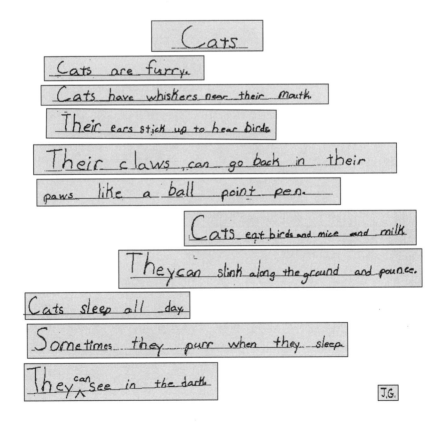

The  completed sheet of pasted information provides the basis for the paragraphs that will make up the writer's informational piece. Most primary students will simply want to title it and copy it to composition paper. Older students, however, should be encouraged to create a web or outline from the paste-up, with an eye toward working out a logical sequence. They may want to collect more information.

Besides introducing young writers to the concept of the paragraph (a clump of related information), this model also shows them that text can be physically moved about in a piece, a very important revision technique.

# Appendix III

## Lesson: Helping young, developing writers write an opinion paper with supporting details.

Children want to be heard. They are no different than adults. Check out the World Wide Web — everyone and his brother wants to be heard. It is important for young students to write about what they think, believe, and consider important. Short opinion papers are a good place to start.

Students in third, fourth, and fifth grade are still very much in the concrete operational stage (see your college notes from Ed. Psych. on Piaget). Until they have worked through a concrete approach to essay — based on personal expertise — they will have difficulty writing about abstract concepts such as honesty, talent, friendship, loneliness, happiness, and such.

Though young writers find it easy to state an opinion, they are not used to providing proof of examples or enlarging on ideas. Use this lesson about providing proof — supporting details — as a model. Invite students to practice this model in their journals or writing notebooks.

The types of supporting details I have described in the Expository Primer can be translated for young writers as follows:

- Definition: *What do you mean?*
- Prove it: *Give a specific detail.*
- Authoritative quote: *Who says so?*
- Narrative vignette: *Tell a one- or two-sentence story.*
- Comparison: *Use an -er or -est word.*

Model how to use these kinds of supporting details by writing your opinion in front of your students on an overhead transparency or easel paper.

First, brainstorm briefly with students to develop lists of out-of-school activities, hobbies, skills. Ask them to star the one they think they could write about today. Then invite young writers **to make a statement** about what they are good at. Model one of your own.

Write your statement. Example: *I am good at quilting.*

Have your students write their opening statements of opinion. Give them a minute or two. Call on some students to share theirs. This will encourage non-starters.

Next, ask the students to **Prove It:** to prove their statement. Any trophies, honors, compliments, prizes, products? Model yours. *I was invited to exhibit my quilts at my town's library.* Call for some sharing so the students who haven't come up with a **proof** can see the possibilities.

Then, ask them, **Who Says So?** Model yours. *My friends and family say my quilts are beautiful and ask me to make them one.* Ask for students to share some of their examples, including the children who now might have a **Prove It.**

Try the **narrative vignette,** or little story. Model one of your own. *Last year I made a crib quilt for my sister's baby. She loved it.* Ask students to share their narrative vignettes.

Finally, ask them to make a **comparison.** Model yours. *I'd rather make quilts than crochet.* Ask students to share their comparisons.

A fourth-grader wrote the following during a modeled mini-lesson:

*I am good at karate. It's a martial art sport. I have a black belt. I won a trophy last year. My coach says I earned my black belt fast. I started taking lessons when I was four. I am better at the kicks than the throw downs.*

Make identifying different supporting details a target skill in peer conferences. Students should try to identify when the writer has used a *Prove It, Who Says So, a good example, How, Why, a comparison, or a little story.* Peer responders simply identify the types of supporting details and compliment the author on their use. If the listener does not hear one, she writes a question mark and the target skill on the top of the peer's paper. This identification-compliment or I-didn't-hear-the-skill exercise is the basis for short, efficient peer conferences.

# Bibliography

American Society of Journalists and Authors. *The Complete Guide to Writing Non-Fiction.* Edited by Glen Evans. Cincinnati, Ohio: Writer's Digest Books, 1983.

Freeman, Marcia S. *Building a Writing Community: A Practical Guide.* Gainesville, FL: Maupin House Publishing, 1995.

Gibb, Carson. *Exposition and Literature.* New York, NY: Macmillan Company, 1971.

Guth, Hans P. and Hausman, Renee V., *Essay: Reading With A Writer's Eye.* Belmont, CA: Wadsworth Publishing Company, 1984.

Jacobs, Hayes B. *Writing and Selling Non-Fiction.* Cincinnati, OH: Writer's Digest, 1968.

Lanham, Richard A. *Revising Business Prose.* New York, NY: Charles Scribner's Sons, 1981.

Power, Helen W. and Di Antionia Robert. *The Admissions Essay.* Secausus, NJ: Lyle Stuart Inc., 1987.

Provost, Gary. *100 Ways To Improve Your Writing.* New York, NY: New American Library, 1985.

Williams, Joseph M. *Style: Ten Lessons in Clarity and Grace.* Glenview, IL: Scott, Foresman and Company, 1985.

Zinsser, William. *Writing to Learn.* New York, NY: Harper & Row, Publishers, 1988.

# If you enjoyed *Listen to This*, try these classroom-tested resources from Maupin House.

### Building a Writing Community: A Practical Guide
### Marcia S. Freeman
*$19.95 / 242 pages / 8-1/2 x 11" / 37 reproducibles / Scope and Sequence Writing Development Chart / For teachers of developing writers, K through grade 9*

New and experienced teachers will appreciate this easy-to-use, comprehensive approach to teaching young writers style and genre characteristics, composing skills, conventions, and the writing process itself. Satisfy the need for young writers to have structure and content while offering them freedom to develop their style, repertoire and voice. Over 350 "What Works" classroom-tested models, lessons, procedures and activities and 37 reproducibles. If you want to create a community of writers who love to write and speak the language of writers, you'll love this book.

### Blowing Away the State Writing Assessment Test
### Jane Bell Kiester
*$14.95 / 118 pages / 8-1/2 x 11" / 41 reproducibles / For teachers of elementary, middle and high school students.*

Jane Bell Kiester is back with more classroom-proven techniques that make you look good. This time, she takes the dread out of the state writing assessment test — and you and your students win!  Four easy steps, and students improve scores. Classroom-proven. Includes 41 reproducible samples.

### Dynamite Writing Ideas
### Melissa Forney
*$11.95 / 124 pages / 8-1/2 x 11" / reproducibles / For teachers in grades 2-6*

If you've ever wanted to integrate a writing workshop into your classroom, but didn't know where to start, this is the book for you. Melissa holds your hand, day-by-day, week-by-week. This book is easy and fun, and it's written for the teacher who doesn't have a lot of time.

### Caught'ya! Grammar with a Giggle
### Caught'ya Again! More Grammar with a Giggle
### Jane Bell Kiester
*$14.95 each / For teachers in elementary, middle and high school*

Can grammar, usage and mechanics be fun?! You bet! Try these classroom-proven classics and watch writing skills improve in just ten minutes a day. Included are day-by-day sentences, with corrections, of funny soap opera stories, with teacher keys, sample tests and special teacher notes.  Each story lasts a year. The first book has three stories; the second one has four. Easily adaptable to meet specific needs of your students. *Caught'ya Again!* also features writing mini-lessons and a complete grammar primer.

Order by check, purchase order, or VISA/MasterCard. Toll free: **1-800-524-0634**. Discounts for teachers with purchases of ten or more books, any combination. Call for shipping and handling information

Authors are available for inservice district workshops.

P. O. Box 90148
Gainesville, FL 32607
jgraddy@maupinhouse.com